Charles W. Bardeen

A Brief Descriptive Geography of the Empire State

For the Use of Schools

Charles W. Bardeen

A Brief Descriptive Geography of the Empire State
For the Use of Schools

ISBN/EAN: 9783337169961

Printed in Europe, USA, Canada, Australia, Japan

Cover: Foto ©Andreas Hilbeck / pixelio.de

More available books at **www.hansebooks.com**

DESCRIPTIVE GEOGRAPHY

—OF THE—

EMPIRE STATE

FOR THE USE OF SCHOOLS

WITH 25 OUTLINE MAPS ON UNIFORM SCALE, 5 RELIEF MAPS, AND 125 ILLUSTRATIONS

— BY —

C. W. BARDEEN

EDITOR OF THE SCHOOL BULLETIN

SYRACUSE, N. Y.
C. W. BARDEEN, PUBLISHER
1895

PREFACE

In the early half of this century much attention was given in New York schools to the study of local geography. It was a time when canals were projected, and the possibilities of water communication between different parts of the State were an engrossing problem. Spafford's "Gazetteer" (1813) gave "a comprehensive geographical and statistical view of the whole State", then the same for each of the 45 counties, and then "a very full and minute topographical description" of each of the 452 town and 4 incorporated cities. Gordon's "Gazetteer" (1836) is so complete in its topographical descriptions that it is on many points still the best book of reference we have. Eastman's "History of the State of New York" (1828), a text book, began with three chapters on "natural geography" of the State. In 1847 appeared a "Geography of the State of New York", an elaborate text-book of 432 pages, by J. H. Mather and L. P. Brockett, with outline maps of the counties.

But local geography gradually dropped out of the curriculum until the Regents began to insert questions upon it. In the first 35 of the Regents' examinations the questions on New York geography amounted altogether to 23 out of 1064, and these were of such general interest that they should be answered by geography pupils in any State of the Union.

But in the 36th examination, for June 6, 1878, a new spirit began to manifest itself. It was asked:

Which is the most westerly of the lakes wholly within the State of New York, and by what rivers does it reach the sea?

Name three rivers that empty into Lake Ontario on the side of New York, and one that empties into Lake Champlain.

The answers were so unsatisfactory that in the next examination (Nov. 7, 1878) these were asked:

What has given to the city of New York its great commercial superiority?

Describe the chief river of New York. To what place is it navigable?

Name the counties in order on the E. side, as far N. as Lake Champlain. Name those on Lake Ontario and the River St. Lawrence.

On what lake is Buffalo? Plattsburgh?

These questions had 19 of the 60 credits allowed, and as they were mostly answered incorrectly hundreds of candidates failed. Vigorous protest was made all over the State, but the Regents replied that the lamentable ignorance manifested only demonstrated the necessity of compelling more study of local geography by the insertion of questions upon it, and since then several of the questions in every examination have been upon this topic. The State and the Uniform examinations have always given prominence to New York geography, so that considerable study of it has been made necessary in New York schools.

The want of a suitable text-book has long been manifest, and the question is not whether a book like this is needed, but only whether this book meets the need. Probably only its actual use in the school-room can fully determine that, but I hope its arrangement and its general features will commend themselves.

Its most marked characteristic is its appeal to the eye. Its illustrations are abundant and have been carefully selected, especially with a view to presenting that aspect of the scene which is typical, distinguishing it from other scenes. Some of the cuts are from photographs taken especially for this book, and many of them appear here in print for the first time. For the photographs of Glens Falls and Howe's Cave I am indebted to Mr. S. R. Stoddard; and for the relief maps to Mr. Walton Van Loan of Catskill.

The series of twenty-five outline maps on a uniform scale is based on the principle of making prominent one thing at a time, which I believe to be exceedingly important. One glance at the map of the Delaware, Lackawanna & Western railway on page 107 will fix in the mind its various routes better than long study of a map on which this road appears with other railways and scores of other features equally prominent. The division of the State into river systems in the map on page 20 is followed all through, the maps of lakes, waterfalls, cities, villages, colleges, etc., being numbered in the same order, that the boundaries of these systems may be kept in mind. Such unusual maps as those of Mineral Springs (page 56), of Indian Reservations (page 69), and of Charitable and Correctional Institutions (page 76) are believed to be valuable. They impress their lessons with very little time and effort, and the information is worth having at hand. So important do I consider these sketchy maps in the study of geography, that I have prepared them for the use of pupils, giving the same outlines that are constant in all these maps, and enabling the pupil to sketch rapidly and during recitation whatever may be the topic of a lesson. These maps are 6x8½ inches, and are sold in pads of fifty at fifteen cents a pad.

In preparing this book I have of course gathered and consulted everything available that has been published. Where extended

quotation has been made I have usually given credit. Of course
I have had constantly at hand the great "Natural History of
the State of New York", on which the State has expended wisely
more than a million dollars, and which should be on the reference
shelves of every union school. The four volumes of Geology have
been of most frequent use, and the previous volumes of the "Geological Survey" have been occasionally quoted.

Next to these I have depended upon French's "Gazetteer of the State
of New York", a thoroughly careful and conscientious work, which
ought to have been better revised than in the hasty edition got out
by Hough in 1868. For the Adirondack region the Colvin reports
have been depended on entirely. I have quoted from Gov. Seymour,
one of the most enthusiastic students of the history of the geography
and history of the State, on pages 82, 83, and the matter on general
topography (pages 13 to 16) is based on an address made by him at
Utica in 1846.

For maps of the State I have depended chiefly on four.

(1) The large Adams & Co. map on copper-plate, and too crowded
to be distinct or always reliable in detail, has the advantage of being
colored by townships, so that for schools in counties where no county
wall-map is published it is on the whole the best wall-map of the
State; but it is more valuable for general impressions at a distance
than for close inspection.

(2) On the other hand, the geologic map of 1894, by W. J. McGee,
issued jointly by the Legislature of the State and the United States
Geological Survey as a basis for a new geological map of the State, is
useless as a school wall-map, being too minute in detail and not
colored so as to represent divisions at any distance. It is still imper-
fect also, as has been mentioned on page 37. But in design it is the
most exact map ever undertaken. So far as I know, it is not yet
published, and advance copies can be got only through some person
in authority.

(3) The railroad and county map, recently issued by the Rand &
McNally Co., has no rival for its special purpose of showing the railroads of the State and the corporations that control them. But it
gives few of the physical features of the State, and does not take much
pains to give these correctly : as for instance it makes Racket Lake,
Long Lake, etc., discharge into the Hudson, thus ignoring the marked
watershed of that region.

(4) In geological divisions I have followed Dr. Hall's map of 1842,
as corresponding with the classification in the "Natural History"

of the State in the school libraries; though a later map was prepared by Frederick J. H. Merrill, director of the State Museum, to accompany the Mineral Exhibit of New York at the Columbian Exposition, and may be obtained of the Regents.

In a book which gives so many facts and figures there must necessarily be errors in the first edition, and I shall rely upon the help of those who use the book to eliminate them. But statistics given should not be condemned because they do not agree with any single printed authority, since nearly every number and statement is give after a comparison of several authorities. So trustworthy a book as Lippincott's "Gazetteer" states in its last edition (1892) that Poughkeepsie is the largest city between Albany and New York, and Elmira the largest city on the Erie between Buffalo and New York; that "numerous steamboats" ply between Dunkirk and other lake ports, and that the Champlain steamers unload their passengers at Whitehall. In heights and distances what should be standard authorities differ lamentably. In the second report of the State Survey it is stated and proved that there is a more accurate map of the moon's surface than of the State of New York. So where authorities differ I have followed those that seemed most trustworthy.

In conclusion I have only to say that the great problem in making this book has been to determine what to leave out. A vast amount of information that was gathered and a good deal that was put into form and into type has been omitted. A good deal has been retained that at first sight might not seem essential to the subject, but which has a place on the theory now so generally accepted of concentration of effort in the overcrowded curriculum of the schools of to-day. I have aimed to make a book that a fifth-grade pupil could use intelligently and with profit. Previous to this grade the work in this subject must be largely confined to local geography and a development of general principles. If this book meets with favor, it is my plan to supplement it by special geographies of each of the counties, much of the material for which has already been gathered. In this book, the matter in the largest type can be gone over in class rapidly, and yet so as to produce a strong impression upon the pupil of the main features of the State geography. With older classes the medium-sized type may be required, and a teachers' class should know the whole book thoroughly. If it interests the pupil nearly as much as it has the author it will serve a good purpose.

SYRACUSE, April 11, 1895.

CONTENTS

CONTENTS

MAPS

ILLUSTRATIONS

NEW YORK THE EMPIRE STATE

STATE·HOUSE·ALBANY

EXCELSIOR

PETRUS STUYVESANT

THE leading position of New York among the United States in population, in wealth, in commerce, and in manufactures is well known, but people do not generally recognize it as geographically the most interesting area of its size in the world. Almost all the natural wonders which singly have given reputation to other regions are found here. Its Niagara is the giant of cataracts, and its Trenton Falls are hardly equalled for placid beauty. Its mineral springs excel in extent of territory and in variety. Its Thousand Islands have no parallel. Its Howe's Cave is not so wonderful as the Mammoth Cave, or its two natural bridges as the great Natural Bridge of Virginia, or its Adirondack region as the Yellowstone Park, or its Ausable Chasm as Marshall Park, or its Watkins Glen as Cheyenne Cañon; its Mount Marcy is not even as high as Mount Washington, and its Catskills are not to be compared with the Alps or the Rockies; its Hudson lacks the traditions of the castle-guarded Rhine, and its interior lakes are not garlanded with the folk-tales of Luzerne. But no other region of the earth so unites this variety of natural attractions as New York. It has the types of almost everything that makes travel interesting, and it has them near together, connected by easy routes of access, and most of them within the reach of every resident. Many of them every resident must see, for the leading lines of railway run by them, and it is only a question whether when he sees them he will recognize their significance. What Horatio Seymour saw in riding from Niagara Falls to New York is told on pages 82, 83. This book is a contribution toward making travel correspondingly interesting to all children who are taught in New York schools.

(9)

GEOGRAPHY OF THE STATE OF NEW YORK

I. POSITION AND BOUNDARIES

The State of New York is situated between 40° 29' 40" and 45° 0' 42" N. latitude, and between 71° 51' and 79° 47' 25" longitude W. of Greenwich. It is bounded on the N. by Canada and Connecticut; E. by Vermont, Massachusetts, Connecticut, and the Atlantic Ocean; S. by the ocean, New Jersey, and Pennsylvania; and W. by New Jersey, Pennsylvania, and Canada.

The northern boundary, commencing in the middle of Lake Ontario, N. of the mouth of Niagara River, extends eastward 175 m. through the lake, midway between the opposite shores, to its E. extremity; thence north-easterly 108 m. through the St. Lawrence River to the 45th parallel of N. latitude; thence easterly 62.75 m. in a gradually diverging line from the parallel, terminating upon Lake Champlain 4,300 feet N. of the parallel.

The Eastern Boundary extends s. 105 m. through Lake Champlain to its s. extremity; thence 17.25 m. s. E. along Poultney River*; thence in an irregular line, but in a generally southerly direction 54.66 m. to the Massachusetts line; 50.52 m. to the Connecticut line; and 81.30 m. through Connecticut to Byram Point, at the mouth of Byram River, on Long Island Sound. From this point the line extends eastward 96 m. through the Sound, very near the Connecticut shore, to the E. extremity of Long Island, including within the limits of the state nearly all the islands in the Sound. This boundary is defined by Chap. 213 of the laws of 1880.

The Southern Boundary extends from the E. extremity of Long Island 150 m. along the ocean to the s. w. extremity of Staten Island; thence 44 m. northward through the channel between Staten Island and New Jersey and through New York Bay and the Hudson to the 41st parallel of N. latitude; thence north-westerly 48.50 m. to a point upon the Delaware at latitude 41° 20' N.; thence north-westerly along Delaware River 78 m. to latitude 42° N.; thence 225.50 w. along the 42d. parallel to a meridian passing through the w. extremity of Lake Ontario.

The Western Boundary, commencing upon the 42d parallel, extends N. 22 m. to the middle of Lake Erie; thence eastward 50 m. to the E. extremity of the lake; and thence N. 34 m. through Niagara River and to the middle of Lake Ontario.

For details as to the boundaries of the State, consult " Report of the Regents of the University on the Boundaries of the State of New York, transmitted to the Legislature, May 28th, 1873 ", 8vo. pp. 362, Albany, 1874; and " Report of the Regents' Boundary Commission upon the New York and Pennsylvania Boundary, with the final report of Maj. B. W. Clarke ", 8vo. pp. 490, Albany 1886.

The extreme length of the State, including Long Island, is 408 miles; excluding Long Island, 340 miles. The extreme breadth is 310 miles. The entire boundary is 1,420 miles long; of which 540 are land and 880 water.

It contains 47,620 square miles of land, and 1,550 of water,—49,170 in all. There are 22 States larger and 19 smaller. It is less than one-fifth as large as Texas (262,290); and 40 times as large as Rhode Island (1,250), which is about the size of Oneida county. It is nearly as large as all England (58,320).

It will be observed that the northern boundary of New York is midway between the Equator and the North Pole, or on the latitude

---

* See Chap. 937, laws of 1879.

of Bordeaux, Turin, and the mouth of the Danube. New York is due w. from Madrid, Naples, and Constantinople; and nearly E. from Pekin. Elmira is directly N. of the city of Washington. New York is nearly N. of Santiago in Chili; Niagara Falls, of Quito, in Ecuador.

It should be noted that the State contains several convenient approximate scales of miles, with which the pupil should be thoroughly familiar.

Thus the following distances are very nearly 50 miles, as shown on the map, and from the lengths of boundaries just given :

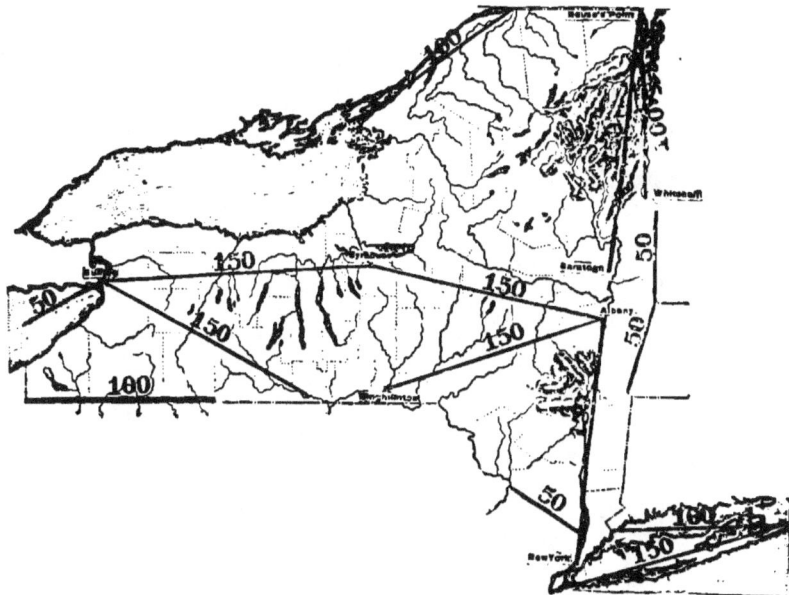

(1) From the middle of Lake Erie to the E. extremity of the Lake (50)
(2) From the Poultney river to the Massachusetts line (54).
(3) From the Massachusetts to the Connecticut line (54½).
(4) From the Hudson to the Delaware river (48½).

The following are approximately 100 miles, also from boundaries :

(1) Through the St. Lawrence to the parallel (108).
(2) Through Lake Champlain to its southern end (at Whitehall) (105).
(3) From the Connecticut boundary to the extremity of Long Island (96).
(4) The southern boundary of Chautauqua, Cattaraugus, and Steuben counties (94).

The following are approximately 150 miles :

(1) Between the extremities of Long Island and Staten Island (150).
(2) New York to Albany, N. Y. C. R R. (143).
(3) Saratoga to Rouse's Point, D. & H. R.R. (153).
(4) Albany to Binghamton, D. & H. R R (142).
(5) Albany to Syracuse, N. Y. C. R.R. (147½).
(6) Syracuse to Buffalo, N. Y. C. R R) 149½).
(7) Buffalo to Elmira, D. L. & W. R.R. (146).

Among the other approximate distances by railway that might be noted are the following :

50 miles—Albany to Pittsfield, Mass., B. & A.,(51) ; New York to Brewster, Harlem (52) : Syracuse to Geneva, and Geneva to Rochester, Auburn branch of N. Y. C. (each 51); Batavia to Canandaigua, N. Y. C. (50).

100 miles—Utica to Watertown, R. W. & O. (92); Syracuse to Rochester, Auburn branch of N. Y. C. (102).

150 miles—Rome to Norwood, R. W. & O. (147); Syracuse to Norwood, R. W. & O. (148) ; Buffalo to Oswego, R. W. & O. (151). The Hudson river is navigable to Troy (151).

It should be remembered that approximations like these *fixed in the mind* and ready to hand when required are of immediate practical value.

II. GENERAL TOPOGRAPHY

General outline—The general form of New York is that of an isosceles triangle.

The Hudson River, Lake George, and Lake Champlain lie in a narrow and rugged valley reaching from the Bay of New York to the St. Lawrence. This is intersected at right angles, about midway, by the valley of the Mohawk. These deep channels constitute the great base lines of our State. Its triangular form corresponds with their courses.

They demand a particular description, for they are intimately connected with the history of New York. They have been the war paths of savage bands and of disciplined armies. They are the scenes of the most interesting and important occurrences in the history of the State and nation. They create our commanding and peculiar relationship with other sections of our country. See opposite map, which gives, besides the rivers, the Champlain, the Erie, and the Black River canals, utilizing their valleys.

The Hudson—The harbor of New York, with its accessory bays, its connection with Long Island Sound, its confluent rivers and its different passages to the Atlantic, excites the admiration of all who study its wonderful adjustments. From this bay you float up the Hudson, past the cliffs of the Palisades, to the rocky fastnesses of the highlands. Here every analogy of nature leads you to look for rocky barriers, but you are borne by the Atlantic tide a hundred miles beyond the mountain chain which elsewhere divides the valley of the Mississippi from the Atlantic coast.

Nothing can be more impressive than the ocean's deep and sullen ebb and flow far down among the great foundations of those stern grey heights. They stand as if arrested here when pressing upon the river current, while north and south they stretch far away in unbroken chains to the St. Lawrence or the Gulf of Mexico. Elsewhere, rivers dash down the steep sides of the Alleghanies ; but where these crowd upon the Hudson, they are cleft sheer down to their very roots An enduring gateway is made through stern portals for ships of war, for vessels deeply laden with commerce, and for iron tracks upon which swift engines drag long trains of cars at the foot of rude cliffs, or through tunnels which pierce their granite buttresses. Ranged for many miles along both banks of the Hudson, had the Alleghanies thrown a single spur across its stream, how would it have changed the course of events in our land ! Impressed with this unbroken ocean current through the Highlands, the observant Indian called it "the river of the mountains".

Lake Champlain—Continuing up its valley, we find lying in its northern depression, separated from the waters of the Hudson by a short portage, the wild and picturesque Lake George and Lake Cham-

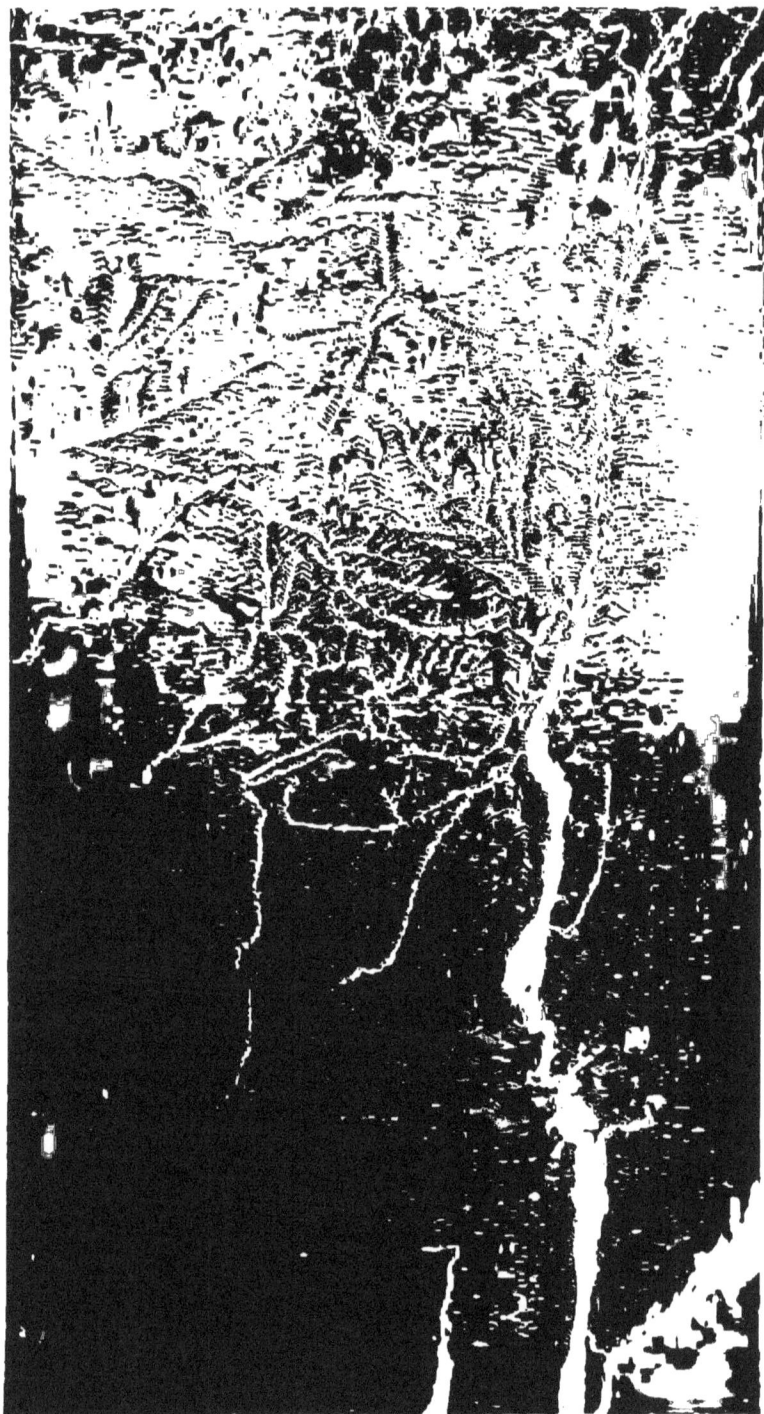

plain. From the Bay of New York to the waters of the St. Lawrence, this great valley divides the eastern part of our State and all of New England from the rest of our confederacy.

In its whole length, its wild scenery accords with its striking legends. Its lower section, along the Hudson, was the stronghold of our country in the Revolutionary struggle. It was the fortress of our liberties. Its rocky points, its mountain heights, its deep ravines, are associated with the history of the war for independence. There is hardly a spot which does not bear the marks of invading assaults or of the intrenched defences of our armies. The waters in the upper valley, which flow to the north, are still more deeply tinged with blood, and have wilder and older traditions of savage contests and of disciplined war. No other part of our continent has witnessed so much of relentless war, of bloody massacres and of fierce battles, as have startled the echoes of its beautiful lakes, and disturbed their wonted quiet and repose.

The Mohawk, which intersects this valley, is intimately associated with it in historical interest and geographical importance. Its valley has extensions to Oswego and Western New York. In passing up its banks from its confluence with the Hudson, we find that at Little Falls it also breaks through one of the ranges of the Alleghanies.

Were the gorge at Little Falls and that at Quebec filled up, all New York and Upper Canada would be again, as they once were, one huge lake.

Connections—In the county of Oneida, it flows through level lands, which, expanding as they stretch away to the west, are at length merged in the great plain of the Mississippi valley. At Rome, the waters of the Mohawk, when swollen by floods, mingle with those which flow into Lake Ontario.

These physical peculiarities of the valleys of the Hudson and Mohawk produce remarkable results. Not only are the waters of the harbor of New York and the St. Lawrence connected by the valley we have described, but turning up the Mohawk, the light canoe of the savage hunter could float into the tributaries of Lake Ontario, and, making a portage around the falls of Niagara, continue on its way through Green Bay, the Fox and Wisconsin rivers, into the Mississippi, and thence up the Missouri into the very gorges of the Rocky Mountains; a distance by the course of streams, of more than four thousand miles. The entire length of the same route can now be traversed by a vessel of burden, by the aid of artificial channels. But a single mile separates the head waters of the Missouri from those of the Columbia river. From the mouth of that stream on the Pacific to the Bay of New York, with the exception of this one mile, there is an unbroken chain of water. The courses of the Hudson and Mohawk, deeply groved into the surface of our State, thus give us the control of the commerce between the 20,000 miles of navigation on the lakes and rivers of the West, and the Atlantic Ocean and the maritime world of the East.

Its watersheds—New York's commanding position is shown by another remarkable fact in its geography. The hills on either side of the Mohawk gradually rise up to elevations which pour from their outward, or northern and southern slopes, the sources of great rivers which traverse other States. The waters which drain from our territories flow by the principal commercial cities of the Union. From Northern New York they run into Lake Ontario and the St. Lawrence, passing by Montreal and Quebec; by the Hudson, which is exclusively a river of our State, into the harbor of New York; from its southeast section into the Delaware, past Philadelphia, into the Delaware Bay; by the Susquehanna past Baltimore into the Chesapeake; by the sources of the Alleghany into Ohio, past Cincinnati and New Orleans, into the Gulf of Mexico. Thus New York enjoys the apparently inconsistent advantages of having the deepest channels for commerce with the West, and at the same time of being at the head of the great valleys of the United States.

This is not a fact of mere geographical interest. It gives the State substantial advantages. It enables us to penetrate with our canals and railroads into all parts of the country, by following the easy and natural routes of rivers. We can go into twenty States and two-thirds of the territories of the Union, without leaving the courses of valleys. No other Atlantic State can make a communication between its eastern and western borders without overcoming one or more mountain ridges.

To recapitulate, one angle of New York rests upon the Atlantic, another reaches north to the St. Lawrence, while the third stretches west to the great lakes and the valleys and streams connected with the Mississippi. New York is placed at the heads of the great valleys, while the Mohawk and the Hudson unite them all and give her command of the commerce of the country.

III. SURFACE

MOUNTAINS

New York lies upon that portion of the Appalachian Mountain system where the mountains generally assume the character of hills and finally sink to a level of the lowlands that surround the great depression filled by Lake Ontario and the St. Lawrence River. The average height of the State above sea-level is about 1,200 feet.

There are two terraces parallel to the shores of Lake Ontario. One, known as the Lake Ridge, from 3 to 8 miles from the shore, may be plainly traced from Sodus Point to the Niagara River. Dr. Hall says of it. "It bears all the marks of having been the boundary of a large lake, and of having been produced in the same manner as the beaches of the ocean." The other, called the Mountain Ridge, 200 feet higher, is some 30 miles from the shore. Most of the central lakes of the State are in this terrace.

Three distinct mountain masses or ranges enter the State from the s. and extend across it in a general N. E. direction.

(1) *The Highlands*—The most easterly of these ranges—a continuation of the Blue Ridge of Virginia—enters the State from New Jersey and extends N. E. through Rockland and Orange counties to the Hudson, appears on the E. side of that river, and forms the highlands of Putnam and Dutchess counties*. A northerly extension of the same range

HUDSON HIGHLANDS

* This range continues the Taghanic mountains. In Rockland county it is locally known as the Ramapo Mountains; in Putnam county, as the Matteawan Mountains.

passes into the Green Mountains of Western Massachusetts and Vermont. This range culminates in the Highlands upon the Hudson. The highest peaks are 1,000 to 1,700 feet above tide.

The rocks which compose these mountains are principally primitive or igneous, and the mountains themselves are rough, rocky, and precipitous, and unfit for cultivation. The deep gorge formed by the Hudson in passing through this range presents some of the finest scenery in America, and has often been compared to the celebrated valley of the Rhine. One range is cleft in two by the Hudson at West Point.

(2) *The Catskills*—The second series of mountains enters the State from Pennsylvania,* and extends N. E. through Sullivan, Ulster and Green counties, terminating and culminating in the Catskill Mountains upon the Hudson. Slide Mountain, shown in this picture, has

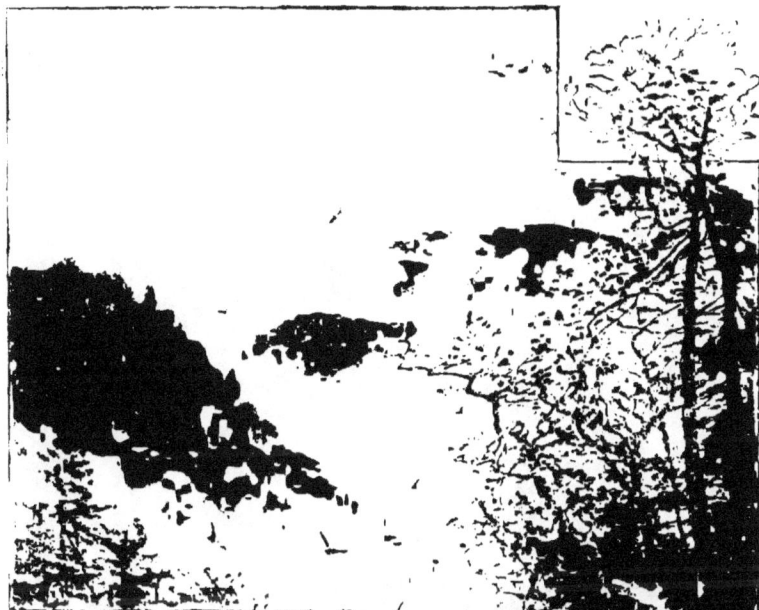

an altitude of 4,200 feet. The lowest parts of Delaware and Sullivan counties are 600 feet above tide.

The Shawangunk (shŏn gum) Mountains, a high and continuous ridge continuing the Kittatinny and Blue Mountains of Pennsylvania, and extending between Sullivan and Orange counties and into the s. part of Ulster, are the extreme E. range of this series. The Helderberg and Hellibark Mountains are spurs ex-

tending N. from the main range into Albany and Schoharie counties Between the Delaware and Pepacton Rivers this range is known as the Delaware Mountains.

This whole mountain system is principally composed of the rocks of the New York system above the Medina sand-

* A continuation of mountains known there as the Alleghany, Laurel Hill, and Broad Top.

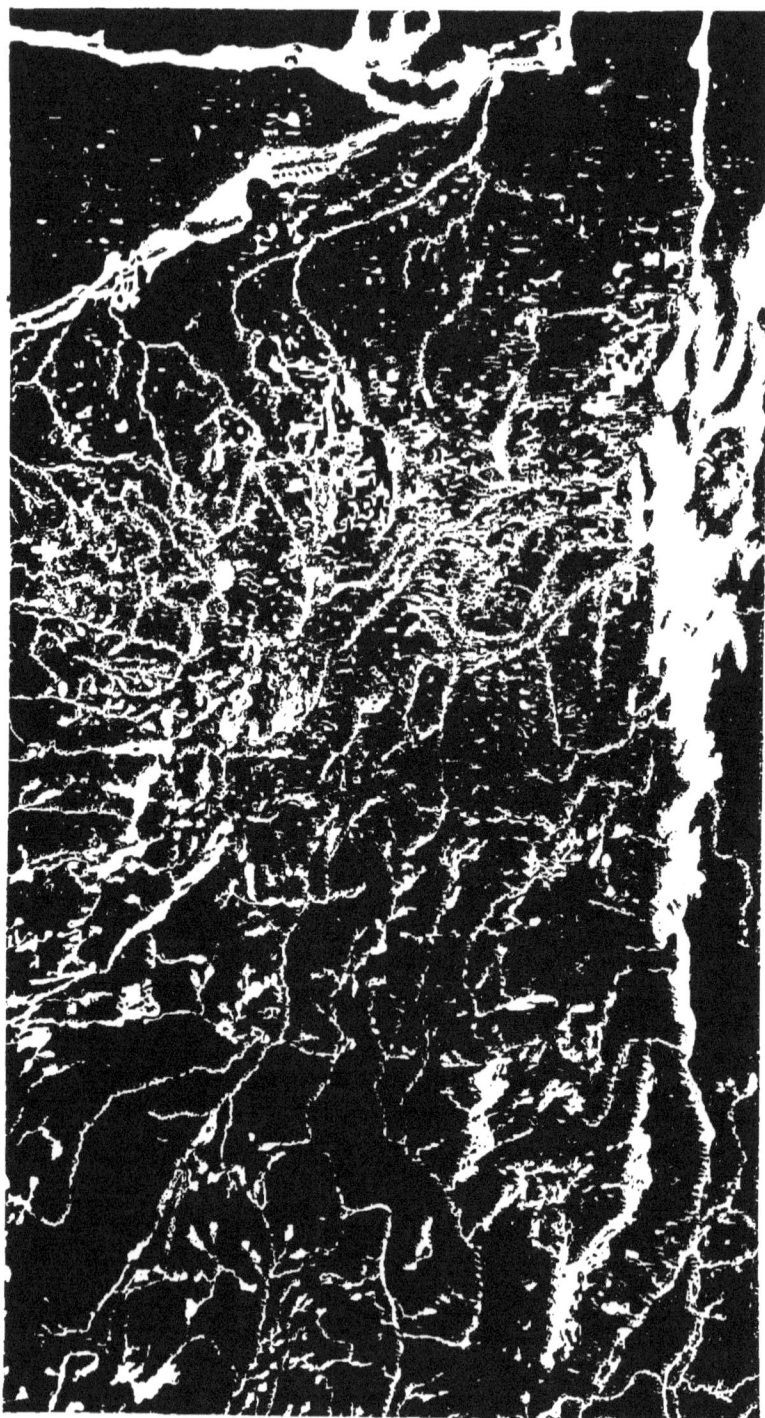

stone. The summits are generally crowned with old red sandstone and with the conglomerate of the coal measures. The declivities are steep and rocky ; and a large share of the surface is too rough for cultivation. The highest peaks overlook the Hudson, and from their summits are obtained some of the finest views in Eastern New York.

(3) *The Adirondacks*—The third series of mountains enters the State from Pennsylvania and extends N. E. through Broome, Delaware, Otsego, Scholarie, Montgomery, and Herkimer counties to the Mohawk, appears upon the N. side of that river, and extends N. E., forming the whole series of highlands that occupy the N. E. part of the State, generally known as the Adirondack Mountain region. Its general character is well shown on the opposite map.

South of the Mohawk this mountain system assumes the form of broad, irregular hills, occupying a wide space of country. It is broken by the deep ravines of the streams, and in many places the hills are steep and nearly precipitous. The valley of the Mohawk breaks the continuity of the range, though the connection is easily traced at Little Falls, The Noses, and other places.

North of the Mohawk the highlands extend N. E. in several distinct ranges, all terminating upon Lake Champlain. The culminating point of the whole system, and the highest mountain in the State, is Mt. Marcy, 5,344 feet above tide. The heights of some of the Adirondack mountains are thus given by Mr. Colvin :

Basin Mt., 4,905	Haystack Mt. 4,919	Mt. Redfield, 4,688
Mt. Clinton, 4,937	Hump (Mt. Marcy), 4,968	Saddle Mt., 4,586
Mt. Colden, 4,773	Lake Tear Notch, 4,355	Mt. Santanoni, 4,644
Mt Colvin, 4,142	Mt McIntyre, 5,113	Mt. Seward, 4,384
Mt. Dix, 4,916	Mt. Macomb, 4,371	Mt. Skylight, 4,890
Giant of the Valley Mt. 4,530	Mt. Marcy, 5,344	Tawahus (Mt. Marcy), 5,344
Gothic Mt. 4,744	Nipple Top Mt. 4,681	Whiteface Mt., 4,872
Gray Peak, 4902	Ragged Mt. 4,163	

The rocks of all this region are principally of igneous origin, and the mountains are usually wild, rugged, and rocky. A large share of the surface is entirely unfit for cultivation ; but the region is rich in minerals, and especially in an excellent variety of iron ore

(4) *The Alleghanies.*—West of these ranges, series of hills forming spurs of the Alleghanies enter the State from Pennsylvania and occupy the entire s half of the W. part of the State. An irregular line extending, as shown in the map, through the southerly counties forms the watershed that separates the northern and southern drainage ; and from it the surface gradually declines northward until it finally terminates in the level of Lake Ontario.

The portion of the State lying s. of this watershed and occupying the greater part of the two southerly tiers of counties is entirely occupied by these hills. Along the Pennsylvania line they are usually abrupt and are separated by narrow ravines, but toward the N. their summits become broader and less broken. A considerable portion of the highland region is too steep for profitable cultivation and is best adapted to grazing. The highest summits in Allegany and Cattaraugus counties are 2,000 to 3,000 feet above tide, and from 500 to 1,400 feet above their valleys. Angelica is 1,428 and Franklinville is 1,580 feet above sea-level.

From the summits of the watershed the highlands usually descend toward Lake Ontario in series of terraces, the edges of which are the outcrops of the different rocks which underlie the surface. These terraces are usually smooth, and, although inclined toward the N. the inclination is generally so slight that they appear to be level. Between the hills of the s. and the level land of the n. is a beautiful rolling region, the ridges gradually declining toward the n.

In that part of the State s. of the most eastern mountain range the surface is generally level or broken by low hills. In New York and Westchester counties these hills are principally composed of primitive rocks. The surface of Long Island is generally level or gently undulating. A ridge 150 to 200 feet high, composed of sand, gravel, and clay, extends e. and w. across the island n. of the centre.

RIVERS

The river system has five general divisions, as roughly shown upon the following map.

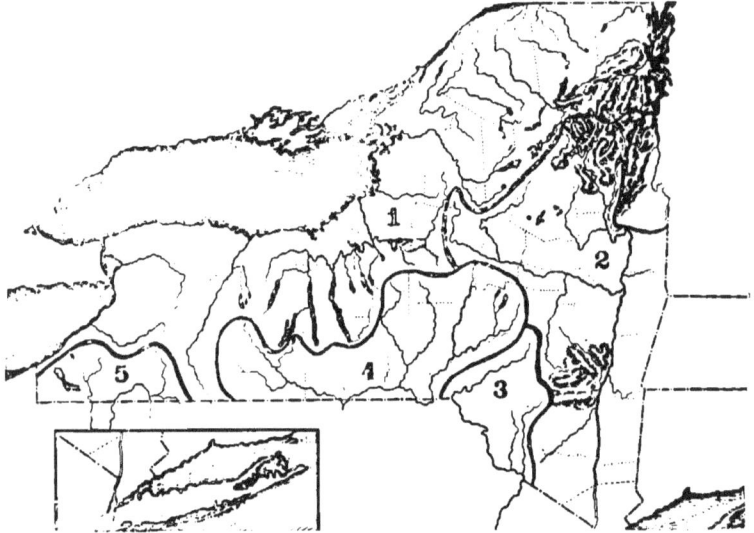

(1) *The St. Lawrence System*, flowing into the Gulf of St. Lawrence.

(2) *The Hudson System*, flowing into New York Bay.

(3) *The Delaware System*, flowing into the Gulf of Delaware.

(4) *The Susquehanna System*, flowing into Chesapeake Bay.

(5) *The Ohio System*, flowing through the Mississippi into the Gulf of Mexico.

(1) *The St. Lawrence System.*—This northerly division has five general subdivisions. (*a*) The most westerly of these comprises all the streams flowing into Lake Erie and Niagara River (2*) and those flowing into Lake Ontario w. of Genesee River (4). In Chautauqua County the streams are short and rapid, as the watershed approaches within a few miles of Lake Erie. Cattaraugus (1) and Tonawanda (3) Creeks are the most important streams in this division. The Tonawanda for 12 miles from its mouth is used for canal navigation. Oak Orchard and other creeks flowing into Lake Ontario descend from the interior in a series of rapids, affording a large amount of water-power.

---

* The numbers in parentheses refer to the map on page 23.

The Cattaraugus is for much of its course wild and picturesque. The Buffalo, Rochester and Pittsburg railway crosses it by a viaduct 250 feet high, and this is 130 feet below the neighboring banks. These high banks are broken here and there by tributary streams, forming in the adjoining roads for 6 or 8 miles what are known as " Cattaraugus breakers", as the road goes up and down like the waves of the sea.

Niagara River (2), forming the outlet of Lake Erie, is 34 miles long, and, on an average, more than a mile wide. About 20 miles below Lake Erie the rapids commence; and 2 miles further below are

Niagara Falls, some views of which are given in the sketches above.

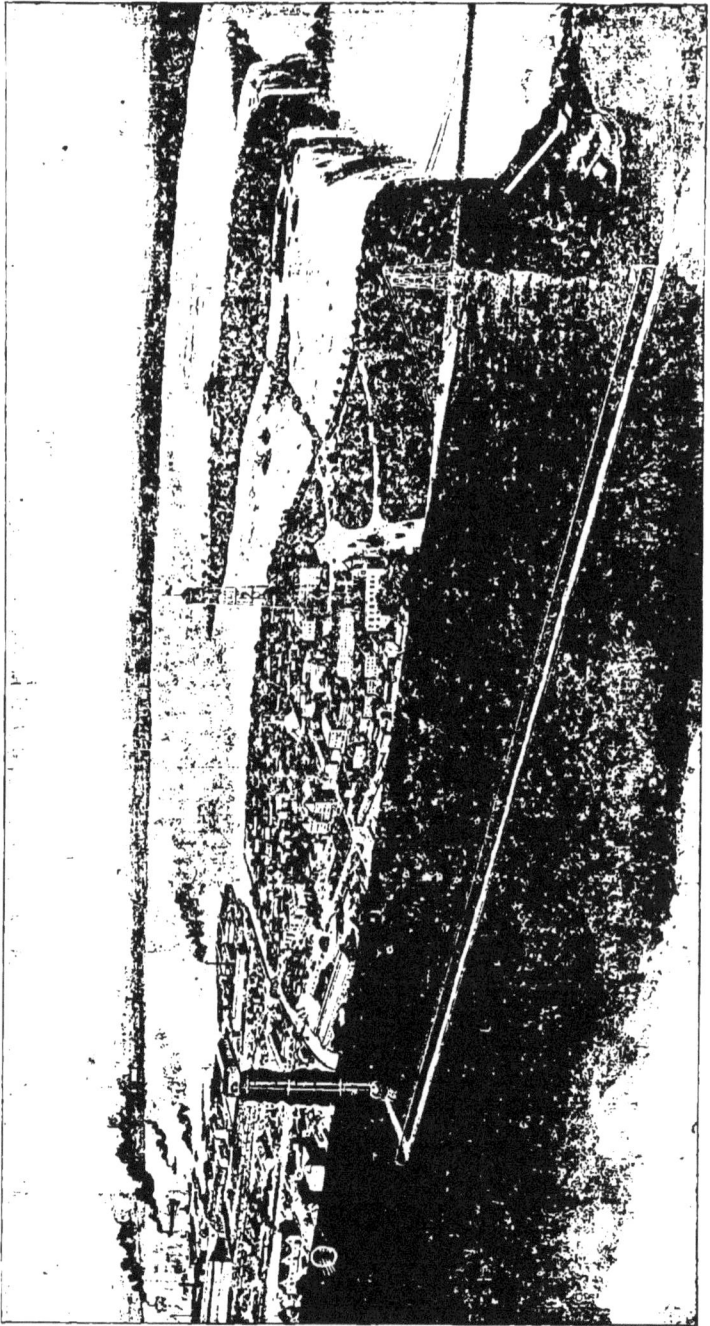

The enormous fall has been utilized by the machinery shown in the opposite picture,* where 125,000 horse-power is already made available.

For 7 miles below the falls the river has a rapid course between perpendicular rocky banks, 200 to 300 feet high; but below it

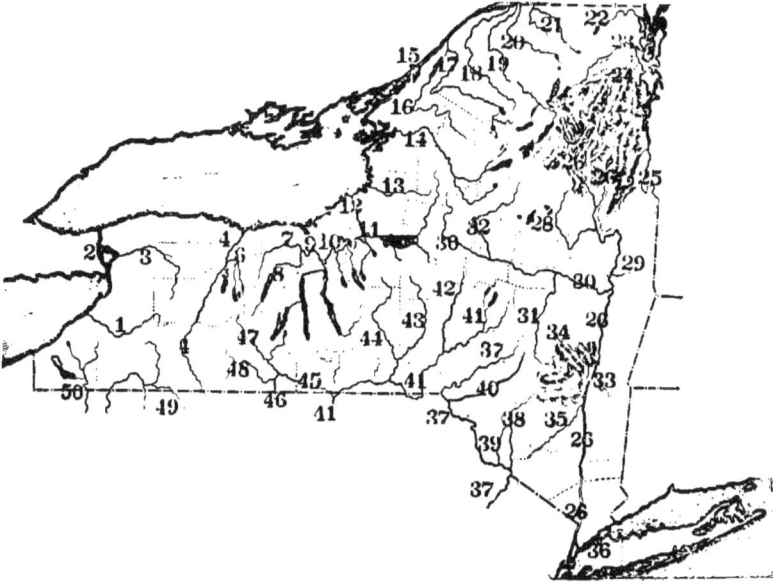

emerges from the highlands and flows seven miles to Lake Ontario in a broad, deep, and majestic current.

(b) The second subdivision comprises the Genesee River (4) and its tributaries. The Genesee rises in the N. part of Pennsylvania and flows in a northerly direction to Lake Ontario. Its upper course is through a narrow valley bordered by steep, rocky hills. Upon the line of Wyoming and Livingston counties it breaks through a mountain barrier in a deep gorge and forms the Portage Falls,—one of the finest waterfalls in the State.

PORTAGE FALLS

Here the Genesee descends in a series of three falls, more than 300 feet in a distance of 2¼ miles.

The water has worn a deep and irregular ravine in the shelving rocks, and the nearly perpendicular banks at the foot of the lower falls are 380 feet high.

The Upper or Horse-Shoe Falls are about three-fourths of a mile below Portageville. The name is derived from the curve in the face of the cliff over which the water flows. For a short distance above the edge of the precipice the water is broken by a succession of steps in the rock, forming a series of rapids. The height of the fall, including the rapids, is about 70 feet.

* Reproduced by the courtesy of The Van Denbergh Laboratory of Chemical Industry, Buffalo.

The Middle Falls are about one half mile further down the river. For 2 or 3 rods above the edge of the cliff the water is broken into rapids, and then in an unbroken sheet it pours down 110 feet into a chasm below, bounded by perpendicular ledges. A cave called "Devil's Oven", has been worn in the rocks under the w. bank, near the bottom of the falls. In low water 10 persons can be seated within it ; but when the river is high it is filled with water, and is only accessible by boats.

The Lower Falls consist of a series of rapids one-half mile in extent, with an aggregate fall of 150 feet. For about 2 miles below the Middle Falls the river pursues a winding and rapid course between high perpendicular walls ; then descends in a succession of steps almost as regular as a staircase, dives under a shelving rock, shoots out in a narrow pass not more than 15 feet wide, rushes down a nearly perpendicular descent of 20 feet, strikes against the base of high rocks standing almost directly in the course, whirls back, and, turning at nearly right angles, falls into a deep pool overhung with shelving rocks. The perpendicular bank on the w. side of the river at one point is 380 feet.

Below this point the course of the river is through a beautiful valley 1 to 2 miles wide and bordered by banks 50 to 150 feet high. At Rochester it flows over the precipitous edges of the Niagara limestone, forming the Upper Genesee Falls; and 3 miles below it flows over the edge of the Medina sandstone forming the Lower Genesee Falls. The principal tributaries of this stream are Conesus (5) and Honeoye (6) Creeks. Honeoye, Canadice, Hemlock, and Conesus Lakes lie within the Genesee Basin.

At the Upper Falls the stream falls a distance of 96 feet over the perpendicular edge of the Niagara limestone underlaid by shale. Below the Upper Falls the river flows 1¼ miles, through a deep ravine bounded by nearly perpendicular sides, to the Middle Falls, where it has a descent of 25 feet. One hundred rods below, it descends 84 feet over a ledge of Medina sandstone to the level of Lake Ontario. The whole fall of the Genesee River within Monroe county is 280 feet. In 1829, Sam Patch, who had successfully jumped 100 feet from Goat Island into the Niagara River, was drowned by jumping from the bank of the Genesee just below the Falls shown on the picture, a distance of 125 feet.

(c) The third subdivision includes the Oswego River (12) and its tributaries, and the small streams flowing into Lake Ontario between Genesee and Oswego Rivers. Mud Creek (7), the most westerly branch of Oswego River, takes its rise in Ontario County, flows N. E. into Wayne, where it unites with Canandaigua Outlet (8) and takes the name of Clyde River (9) ; thence it flows E. to the w. line of Cayuga County, where it empties into Seneca River (10). This latter stream, made up of the outlets of Seneca and Cayuga Lakes, from this point flows in a N. E. course, and receives successively the Outlets of Owasco, Skaneateles, Onondaga, and Oneida Lakes, the last through the Oneida River (11). From where it meets the last-named stream at Three

River Point, as shown in the cut, it takes the name Oswego River (12), and its course is nearly due N. to Lake Ontario.

The flow of water is about 600,000 cubic feet a minute. Three River Point. is 20 miles above Oswego, and there is a fall of water amounting to 75 feet. " This space is taken up by 7 dams erected and maintained by the State. Of these two are situated at Oswego, covering a fall of 40 feet. These dams accord hydraulic privileges equal to 25,000 horse power. But a moderate outlay is required to keep the flow in the river near the average for the year. Of this water supply 75,000 cubic feet are in actual use in Oswego, where a canal is provided for the reception which furnishes 50 runs of first class water and over 17 of the second class. Two dams are situated at Fulton with 20,-000 horse-power. At this point the water privileges are most available, although Oswego has the greater representation of industries. The Oswego River water-shed produces clear cold water, which is perfectly under control of man, no matter what the circumstances or exigences."

(*d*) The fourth subdivision includes the streams flowing into Lake Ontario and the St. Lawrence (15) E. of the mouth of the Oswego. The principal of these are Salmon (13), Black (14), Oswegatchie (17), Grasse (18), Racket (19), St. Regis (20), and Salmon (21) Rivers. The Indian River (16) is a tributary of the Oswegatchie. These streams mostly take their rise upon the plateau of the great northern wilderness, and in their course to the lowlands are frequently interrupted by falls, furnishing an abundance of water-power. The water is usually very dark, being colored with iron and the vegetation of swamps.

St. Lawrence River (15) forms the outlet of the lake and the N. boundary of the State to the E. line of St. Lawrence county. It is a broad, deep river, flowing with a strong yet sluggish current until it passes the limits of this State. In the upper part of its course it incloses a great number of small islands, known as " The Thousand

Islands ". The river scenery upon the St. Lawrence is unsurpassed. The water is perfectly pure and nearly transparent. In consequence of its being fed by the great lake reservoirs, it is never subject to sudden rises, but steadily pursues its majestic way to the ocean, unaffected by the changes of the seasons or other causes. Further down, how-

ever, it has rapid descents at Lachine Rapids shown in this picture, and at Long Sault Rapids.

(*c*) The fifth subdivision includes all the streams flowing into Lakes George and Champlain. They are mostly mountain torrents, frequently interrupted by cascades. The principal streams are the Chazy (22), Saranac (23). Au Sable (24), and Poultney (25) rivers. Deep strata of tertiary clay extend along the shores of Lake Champlain. The water of most of the streams in this region is colored by the iron over which it flows.

Ausable Chasm, through which the Ausable (24) makes its way to the lake. is pictured and described on page 50.

(2) *The Hudson System.*—The Basin of the Hudson (26) occupies about two-thirds of the E. border of the State, and a large territory extending into the interior. The remote sources of the Hudson are among the highest peaks of the Adirondacks, more than 4,000 feet above tide. Several of the little lakes which form reservoirs of the Upper Hudson are 2,500 to 3,000 feet above tide. The stream rapidly descends through the narrow defiles into Warren County, where it receives from the E. Schroon River (27), the outlet of Schroon Lake, and from the w. Sacondaga River (28). Below the mouth of the latter the river turns eastward, and breaks through the barrier of the Luzerne Mountains in a series of rapids and falls. At Fort Edward it again turns s. and flows with a rapid current, frequently interrupted by falls, to Troy. 160 miles from the ocean. At this place the river falls into an estuary, where its current is affected by the tide; and from this place to its mouth it is a broad, deep, sluggish stream About 60 miles from its mouth the Hudson breaks through the rocky barrier of the Highlands, forming the most easterly of the Appalachian Mountain Ranges; and along its lower course it is bordered on the w. by a nearly perpendicular wall of basaltic rock 300 to 500 feet high. known as "The Palisades". See page 14.

Above Troy the Hudson receives Hoosick River

VIEW FROM PALISADES (29) from the E. and the Mohawk (30) from the w. At Little Falls and "The Noses" the Mohawk breaks through mountain barriers in a deep. rocky ravine; and at Cohoes, about 1 mile from its mouth. it flows down a perpendicular precipice of 70 feet, forming an excellent water-power. The principal tributaries of the Mohawk are Schoharie (31) and West Canada (32) Creeks. On the latter are Trenton Falls.

The Mohawk at Little Falls is pictured on page 52, and the Trenton Falls are pictured and described on page 53. The cascade at Cohoes is in full view of the railroad bridge, a short distance below. The Erie canal (see page 43) rises here by a series of 18 locks through the city, to a point 188 feet above tide.

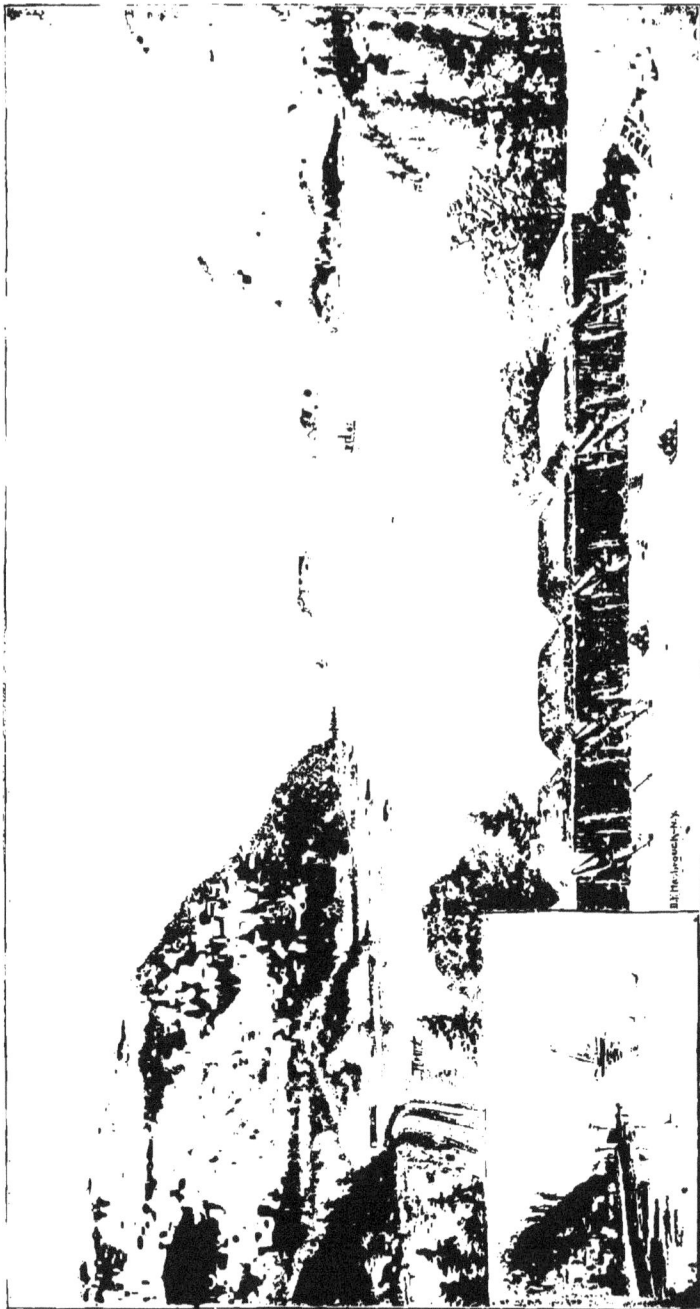

VIEW UP THE HUDSON FROM WEST POINT—NEWBURGH IN THE DISTANCE.

Below Troy the principal tributaries of the Hudson are Jansen's (33),

Norman's Kill (34) and Rondout (35) Creeks. The cut given shows the West Shore railroad bridge over Rondout Creek.

EAST RIVER BRIDGE

South of the Highlands the river spreads out into a wide expanse known as "Tappan Bay".

The western arm of Long Island sound is commonly known as the East River (36), and the Hudson at New York is usually called the North River. Across the East River is the great Brooklyn Bridge, uniting New York with Brooklyn. This is 5,989 feet long. 135 feet above the water, and cost 15 millions. It is suspended by steel wire cables from stone piers 272 feet above high tide, and carries promenades, carriage ways, and railway tracks.

The Harlem River is the narrow portion of tide water separating Manhattan island from the main land. It communicates through Spuyten Duyvil Creek with the Hudson River, and at Hell Gate with the East River. It is spanned by High Bridge, carrying the Croton water to New York, and by Washington Bridge, which cost three millions.

WASHINGTON BRIDGE, HIGH BRIDGE

(3) *The Delaware System.*—The Delaware Basin occupies Delaware and Sullivan and portions of several of the adjacent counties. The N. or principal branch of the Delaware River (36) rises in the N. E. part of Delaware county and flows s. w. to near the Pennsylvania line ; thence it turns s. E. and forms the boundary of the State to the line of New Jersey.

Its principal branches are the Pepacton (40), Mongaup (39), and

Neversink (38) Rivers. These streams all flow in deep, narrow ravines bordered by steep rocky hills.

The picture on the opposite page shows the picture of Delaware and the Neversink at the point where the three States of New York, New Jersey, and Pennsylvania meet.

NEVERSINK VALLEY, NEAR GUYMARD

(4) *The Susquehanna System.*—The Susquehanna Basin occupies about one-third of the s. border of the State. The Susquehanna River (41) takes its rise in Otsego Lake, and flowing s. w. to the Pennsylvania

line, receives the Unadilla (42) from the N. After a course of a few miles in Pennsylvania it again enters the State, and flows in a general westerly direction to near the W. border of Tioga County, whence it turns S. and again enters Pennsylvania. Its principal tributary from the N. is Chenango River (43), of which the Tioughnioga (44) is the principal branch.

The Tioga River (46) enters the State from Pennsylvania near the border of Steuben County, flows N., receives the Canisteo (48) from the W. and the Cohocton (47) from the N. From the mouth of the latter

the stream takes the name Chemung River (45), a view along which is shown in the cut, and flows in a S. E. direction, into the Susquehanna (41) in Pennsylvania, a few miles S. of the State line. The upper course of these streams is generally through deep ravines bordered by steep hillsides; but below they are bordered by wide and beautiful intervales.

(5) *The Ohio System.*—The Alleghany Basin embraces the southerly half of Chautauqua and Cattaraugus counties and the S. W. corner of Allegany. The Alleghany River (49) enters the State from the S. in the S. E. corner of Cattaraugus County, flows in nearly a semicircle, with its outward curve toward the N., and flows out of the State in the S. W. part of the same county. It receives several tributaries from the N. and E., the principal of which is Conewango Creek (50).

The lakes are so closely associated with the rivers of which they are usually mere expansions*, that they might have been treated with them ; but in New York they are so many and form so large an element of its attractiveness, that it seems better to give them a separate heading.

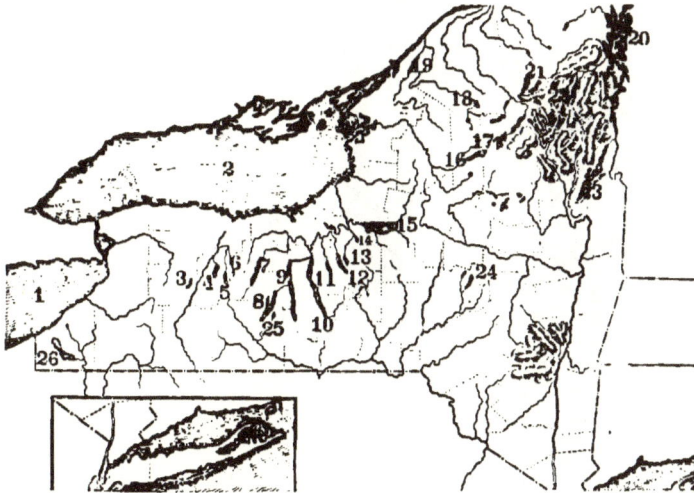

(1) *The St. Lawrence System.*—(a) Lake Erie (1) forms a portion of the w. boundary of the State. It is 240 miles long, with an average width of 38 miles, and it lies mostly w. of the bounds of the State. It is 334 feet above Lake Ontario (2), 573 feet above tide, and has an average depth of 120 feet. The greatest depth ever obtained by soundings is 270 feet.

(b) Lake Ontario (2) forms a part of the N. boundary to the w. half of the State. Its greatest length is 130 miles and its greatest width 55 miles. It is 247 feet above tide, and its greatest depth is 600 feet. Its principal harbors on the American shore are Lewiston, Youngstown, Port Genesee, Sodus and Little Sodus Bays, Oswego, Sackett's Harbor, and Cape Vincent.

The surfaces of the great lakes are subject to variations of level,—probably due to prevailing winds, unequal amounts of rain, and evaporation. The greatest difference known in Lake Erie is 7 feet, and in Lake Ontario 4½ feet. The time of these variations is irregular ; and the interval between the extremes often extends through several years. A sudden rise or fall of several feet has been noticed upon Lake Ontario at rare intervals, produced by some unknown cause.

Silver (3), Conesus (4), Hemlock (5) and Honeoye (6) lakes lie in the Genesee Basin.

Hemlock lake furnishes water to the city of Rochester.

* It is believed that the basis of most New York lakes were dug out by ice during the glacial period.

Canadice lake lies between Hemlock and Honeoye lakes, as shown in the map.

(c) The basin of the Oswego includes most of the best-known inland lakes, which form so remarkable a feature of the interior landscape of the State. Canandaigua (7), Keuka (8), Seneca (9), Cayuga (10), Skaneateles (12), and Otisco (13), all occupy long, narrow valleys, extending from the level land on the north into the highlands of the south. The valleys seem like immense ravines, formed by some tremendous force, which has torn the solid rocks from their original beds in the general level of the surrounding summits down to the present bottoms of the lakes*.

The shores of Canandaigua lake (7) 15 miles long, slope down to the very edge of the water, except at the head, where they rise in steep bluffs to from 300 to 800 feet. Its surface is 668 feet above tide.

Keuka (8), or Crooked Lake, 20 miles long, lies in a deep valley nearly surrounded by steep hills 500 to 800 feet high, and famous like the hills on the Rhine for vineyards and wine-cellars. This bird's eye view of it gives an idea of the general appearance of all these lakes.

---

*The ravines of these lakes, and the streams which flow down parallel to them, are usually bordered by steep hillsides, the strata of which lie in parallel layers nearly level E. and W., and slightly inclined toward the s. Upon the opposite banks the dissevered edges of the strata exactly correspond, showing that the intermediate portions have been torn away. The force that effected these immense changes was probably great currents of water from the N., the direction being determined by the character of the boulders upon the hills, and by the peculiar nature of the drift deposits.

Seneca Lake (9) 36 miles long and from 1 to 4 miles wide, is 416 feet above Lake
Ontario, and 447 feet above tide. It occupies a deep valley, and has a depth in some
places 630 feet. Its shores are generally bold, and from their summits the land slopes
gently and gracefully to a height of 200 to 700 feet above the surface. It is never
entirely frozen over, and the steamers run all winter. The prosperous village of Watkins

lies at its head, as shown in the picture, and near by are Watkins and Havana Glens,
described on pp. 45, 47.

It is connected by the Seneca river with Cayuga Lake (10). This lake is 38 miles

CAYUGA LAKE, AS SEEN FROM CORNELL UNIVERSITY

long, and from 1 to 3 miles wide, and 387 feet above tide. Its greatest depth is 346 feet,
but at the foot it is shallow, reaching out at its mouth into a swampy region known as
the Montezuma marshes. The beautifully rolling shores give way toward the head to
bluffs 700 feet high, cut through E. and W. by rapid side streams that give admir-
able opportunity for the study of the State's geology.

The shores of Owasco Lake (11) are bold and in some places precipitous. Its outlet flows through the city of Auburn, 2½ miles N., which it supplies with water.

As one goes S. upon Skaneateles Lake (12), 16 miles long, the rolling farms at its foot

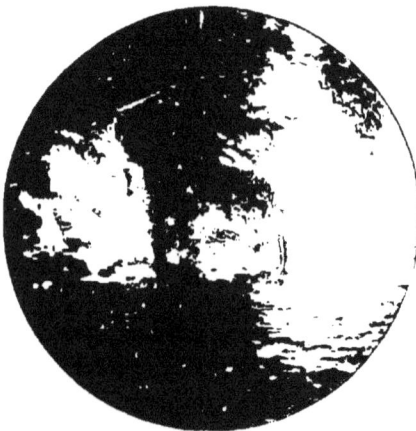

NATURAL VASE, SKANEATELES LAKE

soon give place to wooded hills that rise to several hundred feet. The scenery here is singularly beautiful, making it perhaps the most attractive sheet of water in the State. For miles the shores on the west side present a constantly varying series of nooks, recesses, and moss-clad rocks of fantastic forms. Toward the head the summits decline, and the land slopes down to the water, forming at Glen Haven a rich and lively landscape. By a pipe line 20 miles long Syracuse draws from this lake an inexhaustible supply of pure water.

Otisco Lake (13), 4 miles long, is nearly surrounded by hills 400 to 800 feet high.

Onondaga Lake (14), 5 miles long, lies wholly in the level lands, and is celebrated for the salt springs that are found in two square miles of low, half-marshy ground about its head. Cross Lake, shown to the W. N. W., is little more than an enlargement of the Seneca River. Cazenovia Lake, not shown, lies a few miles to the east. It is 4 miles long and 900 feet above tide.

Oneida Lake (15), 20 miles long, and in some places 6 miles wide, lies like Onondaga in the level lands, being only 191½ feet above Lake Ontario. Considerable land in its vicinity is marshy.

	LENGTH IN MILES	GREATEST WIDTH	ELEVATION ABOVE TIDE	GREATEST DEPTH
Canandaigua.	15	2	668 feet.	Shallow.
Keuka	20	2	718 "	200 feet.
Seneca	36	1	447 "	630 "
Cayuga	38	3	387 "	346 "
Owasco	10	1	765 "	Shallow.
Skaneateles	16	1¼	860 "	320 feet.
Onondaga	5	1	361 "	65 "
Oneida	20	6	373 "	Shallow.

(*d*) The St. Lawrence streams drain the greater part of what tourists

know as the Adirondack region, including a multitude of small lakes, and some such larger ones as Fourth (16), Racket (or Raquette) (17), Cranberry (18), and Black (19).

Moss and Tear-of-Cloud lakes are more than 4,300 feet above sea-level. Blue Mountain Lake is 1800 feet above the sea, and empties through Eagle Lake into Racket Lake.

BLUE MOUNTAIN LAKE

Massawepie Lake is the fountain head of the Grasse (or La Grasse) River (No. 18 in the map on page 23), and near it is the Childwold Park House; while across Catamount Pond, near by, is Gale's, a well-known headquarters for hunters. The upper Racket river, near by, is a favorite camping-ground.

Tupper Lake lies a few miles south-east, still in the St Lawrence basin, while just a little N. of E. are the Saranac lakes, in the Champlain basin, the water-shed being near line of the railroad.

The geologic map of the State (1894) fails to give the stream connecting Upper and Middle Saranac Lakes, and so leaves the Upper Saranac with no outlet whatever.

MASSAWEPIE LAKE, FROM CHILDWOLD PARK HOUSE

This is the region particularly helpful to consumptives, and many invalids remain here the year around.

(7) Lake Champlain (20) receives the water from the closely connected upper and lower Saranac (21) Lakes, and from Lake Placid (22) shown in the adjoining picture, all three famous as summer resorts. It is itself a favorite resort, its steamers offering a convenient route for summer travel, and its numerous islands furnishing delightful summer homes.

The eastern Adirondack region is mountainous, while the western region is mostly low, to some extent marshy. The pictures on these two opposite pages show their contrasting characteristics.

The "North Woods", as most New Yorkers familiarly call them, are at once an attraction and a sanitarium. Within a few hour's ride of any part of the State, they offer to the overworked and nervous dweller in large cities a sudden plunge into the stillness of the forest primeval. As Judge Northrup well says: "To a man whose life is chiefly within four brick walls, and whose every breath takes up some part of the street and its filth, whose daily work is such that his body and health are a daily sacrifice to the necessities of sedentary life,—to such a man there is nothing in the whole range of remedial agents to make him so sound and strong and well and in so short a time, like the two or three weeks he can spare for a trip to the woods."—*Camps and Tramps*, p. 13.

The length of the Champlain valley is 180 miles, and the depth of the lake is in places 600 feet, or 500 feet below the level of the ocean. Its bed is a deep chasm, principally in the primary rocks, formerly the bed of an ancient ocean. It is interesting to note that its tributary streams on both sides bear toward the north.

Among the most interesting of these is the outlet from Lake George, the water of which flows over two picturesque falls as it descends 240 feet in 4 miles. Near where the stream enters the lake are the famous ruins of Fort Ticonderoga, which Col. Ethan Allen captured in 1775, "in the name of the Great Jehovah and the Constitutional Congress."

RUINS OF FORT TICONDEROGA

Lake George (23), or Horicon, 36 miles long, and from 1 to 4 miles wide, is famed for the beauty of its scenery, being often called the Como of America.

"Surrounded on all sides, except at the outlet, by beautiful hills, and mountains of primitive rock, it receives from their springs and brooks an unfailing supply of water that is sufficiently sparkling and pure to justify the name—St. Sacrament—which the lake originally received. At some remote period, this whole region was swept over by a great deluge which left the country far and wide covered with loose earth and gravel, and gave to the lake a floor of beautiful white sand. This, in connection with the crystal purity of the water, renders objects visible at a considerable depth.

LAKE GEORGE

"Only a small portion of the lake is seen at a single view. There is no broad and striking expanse of water. This lake (like Como and Windermere) assumes more of the character of a noble river flanked by highlands. Winding sweetly on its way among the verdant hills, it gradually unfolds its wealth of beauty, surprising and delighting the tourist at every advance by some new and exquisite scene."—*B. F. De Costa.*

It is studded with hundreds of islands. At its south-east end French Mountain rises abruptly some 2,500 feet, and the western shore is bordered by high bluffs. The principal hotel is named from Fort William Henry, surrendered to the French in 1756. On the road to Glens Falls is a monument to Col. Ephraim Williams, after whom Williams College is named, who was killed by the French on Sept. 8, 1755, and is buried where he fell. This entire region is the groundwork of Cooper's "Last of the Mohicans".

(2) *The Hudson System.*—Besides the multitude of small lakes near its source, the Hudson has tributaries farther down from several lakes

at high altitudes, a type of which is Lake Mohonk in the southern part of Ulster county, shown in this picture.

This lake, and Lake Minnewaska, just above it, are shown on the map, page 14, up in the mountains near the northern branch of Rondout Creek. The square-shaped lake on the E. of the Hudson farther down is Lake Mahopac, the pride of the Croton water-shed, 1800 feet above the sea, and a popular summer resort.

(3) *The Susquehanna System.*—The principal lake in this system is
Otsego (24), 9 by 1½ miles, and
1193 feet above sea level.

Cooperstown, at its foot, was the residence of the famous novelist, James Fenimore Cooper, whose stories have made this region familiar the world over. The stage-ride to Richfield Springs is delightful. Views of the lake are shown on page 58.

OTSEGO LAKE

The lake close by on the map is Schuyler's, or Canadarago, 5 miles long.

Little Lake (25) is chiefly interesting as showing the watershed of
that region.

There is a lake at Tully, not shown on the map, but near the centre of the southern boundary of Onondaga County, out of which the water flows to the N. through Onondaga Creek and Onondaga Lake to the Gulf of St. Lawrence, and also to the S. through the Tioughnioga into Chesapeake Bay.

(5) *The Ohio System.*—Chautauqua Lake (26), 9 miles S. of Lake
Erie, but 740 feet above it, and 1,400 feet above the sea, is probably
higher than any other navigable lake E. of the Rocky Mountains.
It is the only large lake in the State that discharges into the Gulf of
Mexico. It has become famous the world over as the site of a summer school and Sunday school assembly, the success of which has led
to a system of home-study in wide use.

CANALS

The natural internal navigation of the State is very extensive.
Before the commencement of internal improvements, the most important lines were, first, N. from Albany, through the Hudson to Fort Edward, thence a portage to Fort Ann, and thence by Wood Creek to
Lake Champlain ; and, second, w. from Albany, by way of the Mohawk,
Wood Creek, Oneida Lake, and Oswego River, to Lake Ontario. Upon
the latter route were portages at several of the rifts of the Mohawk,
from the Mohawk to Wood Creek, and at Oswego Falls.

The two Wood Creeks mentioned are not shown on the map of rivers, page 23. The first rises in French Pond, Warren County, and flowing N. E. through Kingsbury and Fort Ann, empties into Lake Champlain at Whitehall. The stream is naturally narrow and sluggish, but deep, having often 15 feet of water, and hence was of great use in transportation. The second Wood Creek flows through Rome near the Mohawk, and into Oneida Lake through Fish Creek, and thus formed a ready connection between the Hudson River and the interior lakes.

The Erie Canal is 363 miles long, 70 feet broad at the surface, 56
feet broad at the bottom, and 7 feet deep. The descent from Buffalo
to Albany is 568 feet, and is accomplished by 72 locks. The canal
cost more than 50 millions. For its interesting history, see Hendrick's History pp. 139–146.

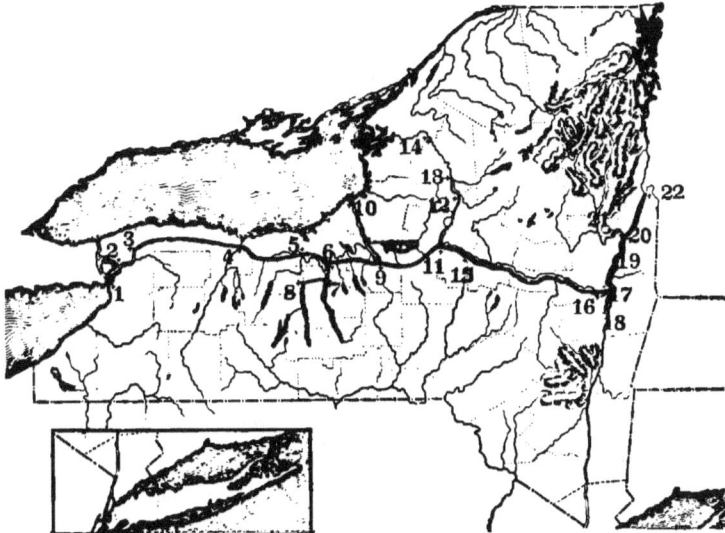

The canal leaves lake Erie at Buffalo (1), follows the river bank to Black Rock, and communicates with the dam at that place. At Tonawanda (2), 10 miles below Buffalo, it enters Tonawanda Creek, follows its channel 12 miles, and crosses thence, through a rock cutting, to the brow of the mountain edge, at Lockport (3), where it descends 55.88 feet by 10 combined locks. It continues thence, eastward, from 1 to 3 miles s. of the ridge road, to Rochester (4), crosses the Genesee upon a stone aqueduct, makes a circuitous sweep across the Irondequoit valley, along the top of a natural range of hills, crosses the Clyde River at Lyons (5), and finally reaches the level of the Seneca River, after supplying 153 miles of the Erie Canal, and affording a large amount of water-power.

ERIE CANAL AT LOCKPORT

It then rises by 2 locks, descends into the Onondaga valley by 1 lock, and then rises by 3 locks to the long level which extends from Syracuse (9) to Utica (15), from whence it descends the Mohawk valley, mostly on its s. side, to the Hudson. Below Schenectady (16), it twice crosses the Mohawk, upon stone aqueducts. It is continued down the bank of the Hudson to Albany (18), where it terminates in a spacious basin. At West Troy it also opens into the Hudson. The total lockages going w. are 612.9 feet up, and 43.5 feet down, or a total of 656.4 feet. The canal is fed by numerous streams along its course, and by 9 reservoirs, besides those upon the Black River Canal, itself a feeder.

The Cayuga and Seneca Canal connects the Erie Canal at Montezuma (6) with Cayuga Lake at East Cayuga (7), and with Seneca Lake at Geneva (8).

About half of the canal is formed by slackwater navigation upon Seneca River, and the remainder is a channel parallel to the river. This canal admits the passage of large boats from the Erie Canal to the head of Cayuga and Seneca Lakes.

The Oswego Canal, extending from Syracuse (9) to Oswego (10), is 38 miles long, and includes 19 miles of slackwater navigation in Oswego and Seneca Rivers, with a towing path on the E. bank.

The Black River Canal extends from Rome (11) up the valley of the Mohawk and of Lansing Kil to Boonville (12), and thence descends the valley of Black River to a point below Lyon Falls (13). From the latter point is a river navigation 42½ miles to Carthage (14), on the line of Jefferson county.

At Boonville (12) the canal receives a navigable feeder 12 miles long, which derives its water from Black River. Length of main canal 36.62 miles, of feeders 12.48 miles, and of reservoirs 12.95 miles. The summit level is 693 feet above the canal at Rome, to which it descends by 70 locks. Northward the canal descends 386 feet, by 39 locks.

The Champlain Canal, extending from the Erie Canal, near Cohoes (17), to Lake Champlain (22), is 64 miles long and has a navigable feeder of 7 miles to Glens Falls (21), with a slackwater navigation 5 miles further upon the Hudson.

A natural water communication, interrupted by portages, extended along the route of this canal, which was used by the natives with their canoes. The canal communicates with the Hudson above the State dam at Waterford by a side-cut with 3 locks. It has 7 locks between the lake and the summit, with 54 feet total lift, and 14 locks, with a total of 134 feet, between the Summit and the Hudson at Waterford. It crosses the Mohawk at Cohoes (17) in a pond formed by a dam 1,700 feet in length, and follows near the w. bank of the Hudson to Schuylerville (19), where it crosses into Washington County by another dam 700 feet long, and continues near the E. bank to Fort Edward (20). Near here it receives the feeder from the Hudson above Glens Falls (21), where there is a dam 770 feet long and 12 feet high. Here it leaves the river and crosses to the valley of Wood Creek, and thence, partly in the bed of that stream, to Whitehall (22.)

WATERFALLS

For Niagara (1), Portage (3), and Genesee (1) Falls, see pp. 21–24.

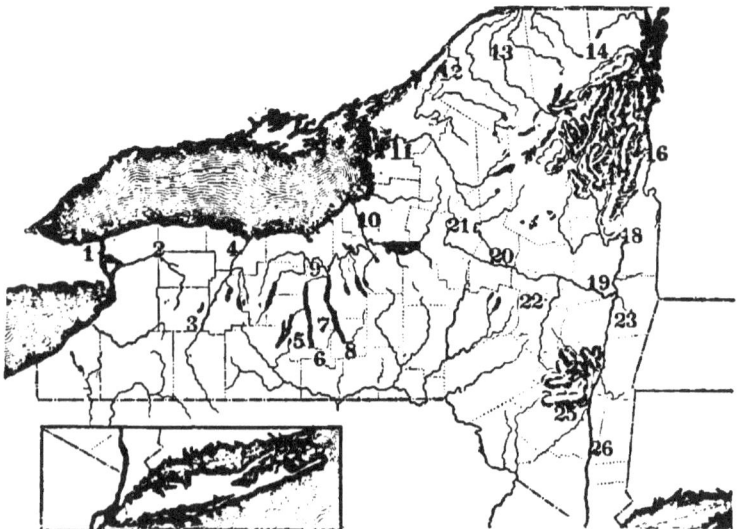

At Tonawanda Falls (2), the creek flows down over the limestone terrace which extends across the southern part of the town of Alabama at a height of 50 to 75 feet.

Watkin's Glen (5) is the most extensive of the many remarkable series of cascades by which the water has worn its way through solid rock in so many parts of the Empire State.

This Glen consists of a number of sections rising one above another

for 800 feet in arcades, galleries, grottoes, and amphitheatres. It extends nearly E. and W. for over three miles, and covers 500 acres.

"It forms the channel for a limpid stream which, bubbling out from mountain springs, threads its sinuous way through gorge and dell, now tumbling madly from lofty heights into the depths of a foam-crested whirlpool, now breaking in shimmering cascades above some pellucid pool shaded by moss-grown rocks; then, winding like a silver thread through the rank leafage of some narrow vale, it flashes in the sunlight

and winds quietly across the level valley, as though, tired from its angry and tortuous passage through the Glen, it was now resting, idly reflecting the sunbeams before taking its final submergence in the cool depths of Seneca Lake, half a mile beyond."

Havana Glen (6) is divided into two general sections, the entrance amphitheatre and the gorges. The former contains within its high banks some 30 or 40 acres, and the latter include a wonderful succession of gorges, waterfalls, cascades, pools, cliffs, grottoes, etc.

The "council chamber" is 100 feet long and 8 to 25 feet in breadth.

Hector Falls, and Lodi Falls, 125 feet high, on the E. shore of the lake, are described with full-page pictures in the fourth volume of Geology, Natural History of the State of New York. Rocky Run, shown on the opposite page, is only one of the multitude of cascades in this part of the State, so common that they are unknown except locally.

Taughannock Falls (7), 190 feet high, is the principal of the cascades by which the creek of that name descends from the plateau to the lake.

These falls have receded about one mile from the lake, and have worn a deep gorge in the yielding shales, with banks 300 feet high. The softness of the rock is shown by an adventure which happened twenty years ago to the author of this volume. He left the steamer at the foot of the creek in the afternoon, and followed up the stream to the falls. These interested him so much that he did not observe how dark it was growing, and he failed to find the path to the hotel on the bank, which he had somehow supposed to be located on the southern side. Underestimating the height, and from the debris at the bottom overestimating the slant, he attempted to climb the southern bank. It was easy at first; then it became harder; finally crevices for the hands and toes had to be plucked out by removing pieces of shale. By

the time he was two-thirds up it seemed impossible to complete the ascent, and as descent was out of the question he considered seriously whether to give it up and drop upon the rocks below. But this involved almost certain death, or, perhaps worse, a night to lie helpless with broken limbs and crushed body. So on the whole he decided to struggle to the last, and after some hours he reached the top. Even then he could not climb over, for the soil projected, and as he held on by the roots every movement he made sent the dirt flying into his eyes and down his back. Finally, seizing the strongest root with his left hand and drawing his body up close, he reached around over the turf with his right hand, seized what seemed to be and proved to be a strong young shrub, kicked out from the bank, and drew himself over upon the solid earth. It was two o'clock when he got to the hotel, and the next day he had not nerve enough left to mount a rock as high as his shoulder. But he had actually climbed in the dark a precipice 250 feet high, much of it by pulling out pieces of rocks with his fingers.

Ithaca Falls (8), one mile from the city, are 160 feet high and 150 feet wide.

ITHACA FALLS

Ithaca has been called the "region of cascades", as there are 96 falls in the near vicinity.

Upon Fall Creek, within the space of 1 mile, are 5 falls varying in height from 44 to 125 feet. The deep gorge through which the stream flows is bordered by perpendicular cliffs. A tunnel 200 feet long, 10 to 12 feet wide, and 13 feet high was excavated through the rock for hydraulic purposes in 1831-32, by J. S Beebe. Upon Cascadilla, Six Mile, and Buttermilk Creeks are also successions of fine cascades, within the limits of the town. At Buttermilk Falls the water rushes down at an angle of about 45 degrees, in a sheet of white foam, the appearance of the water furnishing a name to both the cascades and the stream. In all these falls the soft and yielding shales form a declining surface, while the hard and compact limestone remains perpendicular.

The deep ravine of Fall Creek borders the grounds of Cornell University, and the Cascadilla ravine is at the south-west corner of the campus, uniting with the view of Cayuga Lake already spoken of (page 35) to give the college a picturesqueness of location that is unrivalled.

At Seneca Falls (9), the Seneca River falls 51 feet, furnishing an abundance of water power.

At Oswego Falls (10), the river, which drains more than 7,000 square miles, furnishes enormous water-power. See page 25.

At Natural Bridge (not numbered on the map, but upon the Indian River just as it passes out of Lewis County), when the stream is low the water passes through a fissure 15 feet wide in the limestone under the road, and has formed grottoes that may be entered for some distance.

The Black River Falls (11), at Watertown, are the most abrupt of

the series of cascades by which the river drops 480 feet in passing through the county.

The rapid fall of the river through Jefferson County prevents continuation of the navigation of the Black River to Carthage already spoken of (page 44). The High Falls at Lyon Falls (13 on map, page 43) are 63 feet high, and a glimpse of them may be had from the railway train.

Rensselaer Falls (12) and Brasher Falls (13) have given names to small villages; the latter is now known as Winthrop.

At the Saranac Falls (14) the river falls some 50 feet in passing through a gorge 1¼ miles long, with an average width of 50 feet, and a depth of from 20 to 30 feet. In its general character this gorge resembles Ausable chasm, described on the next page. Another remarkable gorge of this kind at Flat Rock, on the Canadian boundary 16 miles w. from Champlain, is 300 feet deep and 16 rods wide. On the Chateaugay River, a mile above the village, there is a ravine 200 feet deep, with a fall of 50 feet.

Indian Pass, between Mt. Mac Intyre and Wallface Mountain, has the mountain on one side at an angle of 45°, and on the other for more than a mile a vertical wall 800 to 1200 feet high. The western branch of the Au Sable River breaks through the mountains at Willmington Notch, with Mt. Whiteface on one side rising thousands of feet almost perpendicularly, while on the other are the abrupt, rugged crags of another precipice

At Ausable Chasm (15), the river breaks through the Potsdam sand-stone in a gorge 2 miles long and 100 feet deep.

The hardness of the rock makes this chasm more remarkable than those in the central part of the State, where the cutting has been done through soft shale and slate.

From the face of the cliff the river has worn back a ragged and irregular channel in the solid sandstone for a distance of 2 miles and to the depth of 100 to 130 feet. The rocks that border it are perpendicular, and in some places overhanging, so that the water can scarcely be seen from the banks above. At several points this ravine is compressed to a width of less than 30 feet. The river plunges into the chasm in a perpendicular descent of 70 feet, and struggles through the tortuous channel, foaming, whirling, and eddying over its rocky bed. It has been aptly called "the Yosemite in miniature". The tops of the banks are fringed with cedars whose somber shadows deepen the mysterious grandeur.

AUSABLE CHASM

At Ticonderoga (16) the outlet of Lake George descends 150 feet in the course of 1¼ miles, and as the water never freezes and is unvarying in quantity, it furnishes excellent water power. See page 40.

On Stone Bridge Creek (17) is a natural bridge.

The stream, after falling into a basin, enters a passage in two branches under a natural arch 40 feet high and about 80 broad, and emerges in a single stream from under a precipice 54 feet high, 247 feet from its entrance. This bridge is described in Morse's Geography (1796) as follows: "In the county of Montgomery is a small, rapid stream emptying into Schroon Lake, w. of Lake George ; it runs under a hill, the base of which is 60 or 70 yards in diameter, forming a most curious and beautiful arch in the rock, as white as snow. The fury of the water and the roughness of the bottom, added to the terrific noise within, have hitherto prevented any person from passing through the chasm."—*Am. Univ. Geog.*, 503.

It is thus described in Watson's " Military and Civil History of the County of Essex County " (8:512, 1869) :

Two very remarkable subterranean passages in the town of Schroon near Paradox lake are worthy of examination. The first of these forms the channel of a small rivulet, by a natural perforation of some hundred feet through the massive rock, 10 or 15 feet below the surface, over which passes the public road, as if by an artificial bridge. The other, which I find referred to in early works on the topography of this region, is a highly curious and interesting exhibition. The explorer enters a lofty arch, several feet below the surface, carved out of the solid rock. It presents, at some points, the appearance of nearly an exact gothic structure, and at others, broken and ragged sides and canopy. This dark and gloomy cavern extends a number of rods, and is from 4 to 12 feet in width, and 10 to 15 in height. It constitutes the sluice way of a large stream, which propels a mill just above the entrance, and foams and dashes through the rocky and precipitous descent.

Though the Hudson rises in the most mountainous part of the State and descends in 150 miles nearly 4,000 feet, its highest falls are at Luzerne, just below the mouth of the Sacondaga, where the river leaps 60 feet over a ledge of gneiss.

At Glens Falls (18) the fall is 50 feet. For Cohoes (19) see page 27.

Below Glens Falls (shown in the cut above) is a small island, through which is a cave extending from one channel to the other. " When the stream is full the sight is magnificent and one that well repays the trouble of a journey. The bed and walls of the river are composed of blue, fossiliferous limestone, and the scenery is bold and striking. The admirers of Cooper must not fail to explore the falls and visit the cave under the rocks below, where the novelist lays the most thrilling scenes depicted in *The Last of the Mohicans*. It was in this cave that Hayward and Cora found refuge ; where David struck his pitch-pipe, and sang the ' Isle of White ' to the chiming of the music of the falls."—*B. F. De Costa.*

At Little Falls (20), already referred to on pages 15, 19, 27, and shown in the picture on the opposite page, the hills on each side of the river are masses of naked rock, rising nearly perpendicular to a height of 500 to 600 feet.

Trenton Falls (21), sometimes known as the Kauy-a-hoora, are made up principally of 6 cascades, with an aggregate fall of 312 feet. The

ravine is 2 miles long, and the banks are in places 150 feet high.

N. P. Willis thus described the falls in his story " Edith Linsey " :

Most people talk of the *sublimity* of Trenton, but I have haunted it by the week together for its mere loveliness. The river, in the heart of that fearful chasm, is the most varied and beautiful assemblage of the thousand forms and shapes of running water that I know in the world. The soil and the deep-striking roots of the forest terminate far above you, looking like a black rim on the enclosing precipice; the bed of the river and its sky-sustaining walls are of solid rock, and, with the tremendous descent of the stream—forming for miles one continuous succession of falls and rapids—the channel is worn into curves and cavities which throw the clear waters into forms of inconceivable brilliancy and variety. It is a sort of half twilight below, with here and there a long beam of sunshine reaching down to kiss the lip of an eddy, or form a rainbow over a fall, and the reverberating and changing echoes,

       " Like a ring of bells whose sound the wind still alters,"

maintain a constant and most soothing music varying at every step with the varying phase of the curtain. Cascades of from 20 to 30 feet, over which the river flies with a single and hurrying leap (not a drop missing from the glassy and bending sheet), occur frequently as you ascend; and it is from these that the place takes its name. But the falls, though beautiful, are only peculiar from the dazzling and unequalled rapidity with which the waters come to the leap. If it were not for the leaf which drops wavering down into the abysm from trees apparently painted on the sky, and which is caught away by the flashing current as if the lightning had suddenly crossed it, you would think the vault of the steadfast heavens a flying element as soon.

Howe's Cave (22), sometimes called the Otsgaragee Cavern, is a remarkable series of subterranean chambers.

The entrance is from the Pavilion Hotel. An irregular, circular opening in the limestone, through which we pass by a level path, brings us at once into an atmosphere of about 55 degrees. We soon come to the "Reception Room", some 40 feet wide and 15 feet high, ornamented with stalagmites. Near by, up an ascending path, is another large room called the "Bridal Chamber", from the wall of which extend huge stalagmites, known as "Washington's Epaulet" and "Lady Washington's Hood", bearing a most striking resemblance to the objects they are named after. The room is ornamented by a circular dome, so high that the light of the lamp does not render its top visible. Next comes a gallery 75 feet high, in the "Giant's Chapel", above the main path which traverses all the while a spacious hall from 15 to 20 feet high; and the "Straight and Narrow Way", some 3 or 4 feet wide at the bottom, while at the height of a man's head there is just room for the head to pass through. The "Pool of Siloam" comes down a gentle incline and forms a whirlpool, disappearing in some cavity below. Through the entire length stalagmites of the most fantastic shapes ornament the walls, while overhead stalactites hang from the roof like icicles.

The "Elephant's Head" and "Indian Dugout" are passed, and then comes the "Haunted Castle", a large circular chamber, having a niche at one side just wide enough to admit a man's body.

Near by is the "Music Room", where musical tones appear to be never done echoing, but go dancing gaily about, returning again and again, filling the air with harmony.

We are now something over a mile from daylight, and enter a boat. Pushing out on a miniature subterranean lake, ¼ mile long, we sail under a limestone arch, the sides of which are ornamented with fantastic shapes in *bas relief*, resembling divers objects.

Beyond the lake is the "Yo Semite Valley", a deep cañon along the edge of which we creep 50 feet above the stream. Soon afterward the course, which seem to have been nearly straight thus far, is suddenly blocked by a solid wall. From this point a passage as yet unexplored leads to the left, forming nearly a right angle with that which we have been following up. We take the passage to the right, through the "Winding Way", 80 rods long, and only wide enough to pass through, forming a long series of "S's", so that one can hardly see a person in any portion of it three feet ahead. The walls, as throughout the entire course, are smooth as glass, though rigid and corniced with wonderful regularity. At the end of this crooked passage are the "Devil's Gateway" and the "Silent Chamber".

"Fat Man's Misery" is a narrow passage in which poor old Jack Flagstaff would surely have struck fast, and a passage through which we are obliged to crawl leads to the "Rotunda", the greatest wonder of all, a circular room 25 feet in diameter, and 300 feet high.

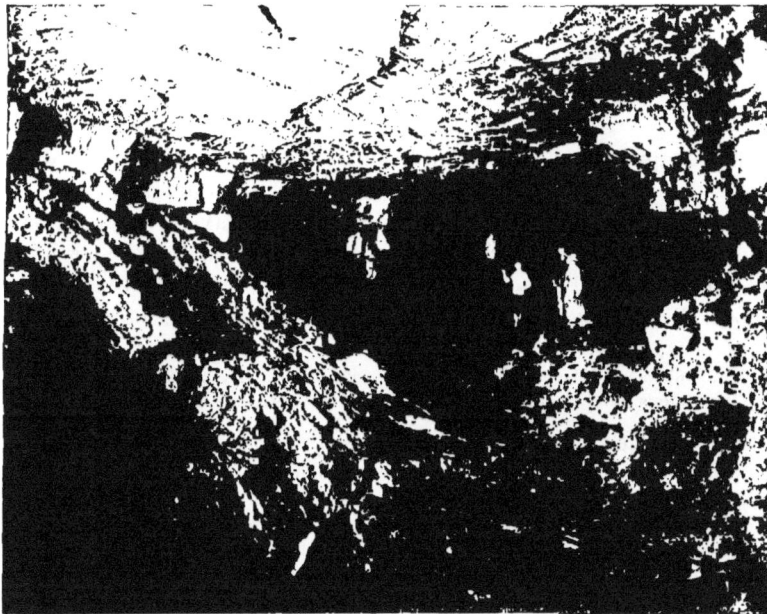

This fitly ends our mysterious journey. A brisk walk of an hour brings us back to daylight once more.

This view of the interior of the cave is reproduced by permission from one of a beautiful series of photographs published by S. R. Stoddard Glens Falls.

At Poestenkill (poos-ten-kill) Falls (23) the river falls some 80 feet. One mile w. is a spring of some local celebrity for the cure of cutaneous diseases

At Kaaterskill Falls (24), the waters from the two lakes and from Spruce Creek combine a short distance from the amphitheatre of rock, and plunge over the projecting 70 feet of massive roofing to the natural cavern beneath, a clear fall of 180 feet. The stream then passes a few yards over smooth rock, and takes another plunge of 80 feet.

High Falls (25), on the Rondout ; and Wappinger's Falls (26) of 75 feet at the head of navigation in the creek of the same name, give names to villages.

MINERAL SPRINGS

The Empire State is remarkable for the number and the variety of its mineral springs. Dr. Beck's report on the mineralogical and chemical department of the Geological Survey gave in 1838 a tabulated list of 148, in 40 of the 57 counties into which the State was then divided ; and these did not included many of those now best known, like the Deep Rock of Oswego, and the Hathorn of Saratoga.

His table classed them thus :

acidulous chalybeate	2	nitrogen	2
acidulous saline chalybeate	17	petrifying	14
brine	24	saline	3
carburetted hydrogen	1	sour	1
chalybeate	6	sulphureous	64
inflammable gas	13	thermal	1

No doubt fully twice as many in the State are now locally recognized as having medicinal value, and many more have interest for the naturalist. During the three years that the author of this volume travelled about the State he learned to ask, if he had an hour to spare, not whether there was something of the sort near by, but what and where it was. In this place, however, it is possible to mention only some of those most widely celebrated.

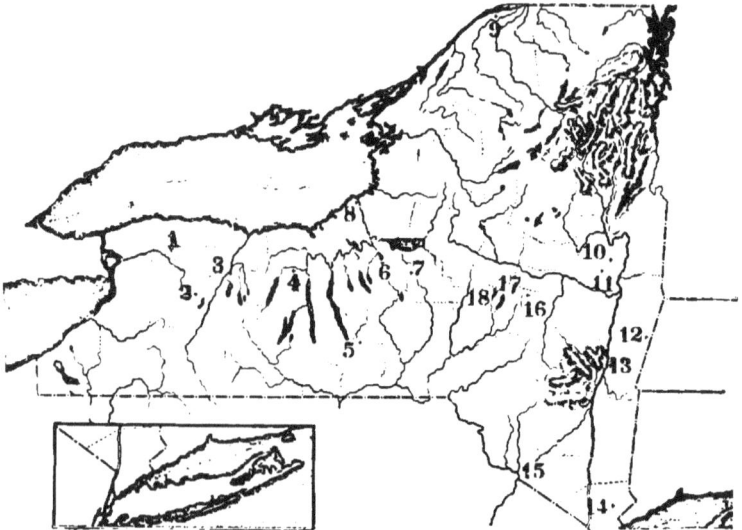

The salt springs at Warsaw (2) have become a formidable rival in the manufacture of salt to those at Syracuse (6).

The miles of wooden salt-vats at the head of Onondaga Lake attract the eye of the visitor approaching Syracuse from the west. Here the brine pumped from wells and distributed by pipes is evaporated by exposure to the sun, the huge covers on wheels being pushed off whenever the sun shines. There are acres too of salt sheds with tall chimneys, in which the brine is evaporated in iron kettles heated by coal. This latter process produces fine salt, while the solar evaporation produces rock salt, in larger crystals. Salt manufacture was once the greatest industry of Syracuse, but has now become unprofitable, owing to the working of wells in Michigan where the brine is twice as strong, and where the kettles can be heated by sawdust from the enormous lumber-mills.

The salt springs at Salt Springville (17), near Cherry Valley, are interesting as showing the eastern limit of these springs, which occur frequently in the region from these W. to Genesee County, and from Broome County N. to Lake Ontario, a region 170 miles by 80. Many of these were formerly worked to a profit, especially those at Montezuma.

An interesting account of them is given in Dr. Beck's Report on the mineralogical and chemical department of the Geological Survey, 1838, above referred to.

The sulphur springs at Avon (3) are visited by many invalids. Clifton Springs (4) contains a celebrated sanitarium. The water incrusts with sulphur the stones that it flows over. At the Massena Springs (9), saline and sulphuric, a hotel was built for invalids as early as 1848.

In the town of Alabama (1) there are 9 springs within a circle of 50 rods, no two of them alike. The Slaterville spring (5) is magnetic. The Chittenango springs (7) are of a saline sulphuric character. In the vicinity are "petrifying" springs, which convert vegetable matter into carbonate of lime, leaving the structure of the plant entire. The Deep Rock spring at Oswego (8) is underneath the Doolittle Hotel. The water is highly esteemed, and is sent in bottled form all over the country.

At Chateaugay, Franklin County, nitrogen springs send out from white sand a flow of water sufficient to turn a mill wheel.

Saratoga Springs (10) is one of the great summer resorts of the world, and contains more capacious and finer hotels of this kind than any of its rivals. There are a score of the springs, greatly differing in character, and some of them are famous the world over.

Its natural attractions and its hotel accommodations have made it a favorite meeting-place for political and educational conventions. To accommodate these gatherings a large auditorium has been erected, seating 5,000 persons.

AUDITORIUM, SARATOGA

The springs at Ballston Spa (11) used to be greatly frequented, but are now neglected in favor of their more fashionable rivals 6 miles N. Lebanon Springs (12) contains a warm nitrogen spring, with several hotels, one accommodating 400 guests. There is a Shaker village near by. The Columbia White Sulphur Springs (13) are 5 miles from Hudson. The Chappaqua (14) sulphur springs have some local celebrity, and there are several springs of different properties near Guymard (15), from which is taken the view of the Neversink river shown on page 31.

The Sharon Springs (16) contain sulphur, magnesia, etc., and are held in high repute.

The Richfield Springs (19) have a wide reputation for the cure of rheumatism and skin diseases, and the hotels and beautiful drives give the village general recognition as a fashionable summer resort.

The views of Richfield Springs on the opposite page include glimpses of Candarago and Otsego lakes.

In this connection should be mentioned the oil-wells of New York, as the petroleum region of Pennsylvania reaches over into Cattaraugus and Allegany Counties. Springs of natural gas or carburetted hydrogen have been found in Albany, Ontario, and other Counties, and at Gasport in Niagara County; while the village of Fredonia in Chautauqua County has been lighted by it since 1821.

ISLANDS

Long Island (4) is 120 miles long and its greatest width is 24 miles.

It is one of a chain of Islands belonging to New York, reaching at Fisher's Island (1) nearly to the Connecticut shore.

It is separated from Connecticut and Rhode Island by Long Island Sound, "the American Mediterranean," which is in places 20 miles wide, but is shallow, varying in depth from 75 to 200 feet.

Geologically the island is interesting, consisting mostly of an immense morainal deposit of glacial drifts, containing a remarkable number of large boulders.

A range of hills from 150 to 384 feet above sea level extends some 60 miles along its northern side.

One of its little lakes situated almost in the centre of the island, Ronkonkoma, has periodical increase and decrease of waters every four years.

The northern coast is broken by important bays, such as Glen Cove, Oyster Bay, Huntington Bay, Smithtown Bay; while along the southern coast stretches a remarkable series of lagoons, formed by a line of dunes at the most a mile wide, such as Fire Island (5), Oak Island Beach, Jones Beach, Long Beach, to the w. of Fire Island in the order named.

The bay N. of Fire Island (5) is known as the Great South Bay, 40 miles long, which furnishes the "Blue Point" oysters, and employs 1500 fishermen.

Peconic Bay which divides the eastern end, is 30 miles long. It is often divided into Greater and Smaller Peconic and Gardiner's Bays, and Gardiner's Island (2) lies between Montauk Point and Plumb Island, just above it.

Shelter Island (3), including 8000 acres, forms a township by itself.

The entire eastern end of the island, including nearly all of Kings county, is now included in the city of Brooklyn. Coney Island, separated from the shore only by a narrow stream, is the southwestern point of the county, as shown on the map. It has become a famous summer resort.

Other of the principal towns are Long Island City, Garden City, Flatbush, Flushing, Hempstead, Jamaica, Oyster Bay, North Hempstead, Huntington, Brookhaven, Riverhead, Southampton, and Southold.

LONG ISLAND CITY is the terminus of the Long Island railroads, and will soon be connected with New York by a huge bridge, as described on page 61.

Garden City was founded by the late A. T. Stewart, who paid some $400,000 for the site, and erected buildings costing several times as much.

Flushing is on Flushing Creek, an outlet of Flushing Bay. It is largely a suburban residence town, but has manufactures of silk, india-rubber, tin, etc.

Jamaica has been designated as the site of a normal school. Riverhead has mills and manufactures of various kinds. Sag Harbor is the eastern terminus of the Long Island R.R., and has a line of steamers to New York.

Staten Island (6) is 14 miles by 8, and forms a county by itself, including 3 or 4 small islands close by. It is separated from New Jersey by the Arthur Kil or Staten Island Sound, and by the Kil van Kull. The bay between Staten Island and Long Island is known as The Narrows.

It is mainly a residence district of New York City, but the oyster trade employs a good many people, and there are some manufactories. On Staten Island is the quarantine headquarters, where all foreign vessels are stopped for inspection; and further up the harbor is Bedloe's Island, with the Statue of Liberty, shown in the cut on page 92.

ELLIS ISLAND

Further along, toward the New Jersey shore, is Ellis Island, where foreign immigrants are received and examined.

Nearer New York is Governor's Island, a station for United State troops. The picture of the fort here given is of Castle William in the north-west corner of this island, which also appears in the left lower corner of the picture of Manhattan Island on the next page.

Manhattan Island (7), 13 miles long, is a part of New York City.

It has the Hudson River on the w., the Harlem on the n., and the East River on the s. and e.

Besides the Brooklyn Bridge, shown in the cut and already described (page 29), it will soon have another communication with Long Island by a bridge now building, connecting the Third Avenue Elevated Railway with the Long Island Railroad, by way of Blackwell's Island, shown in the cut. This bridge is 135 feet above the water and has three spans : 846 feet from New York to the Island, 615 feet across the Island, and 846 feet from the Island to Long Island City. It is to cost 8 millions, beside the cost of the terminal stations. It has 4 railway tracks, with carriage ways on each side.

New York City includes Ward's Island, Blackwell's Island, and Randall's Island in

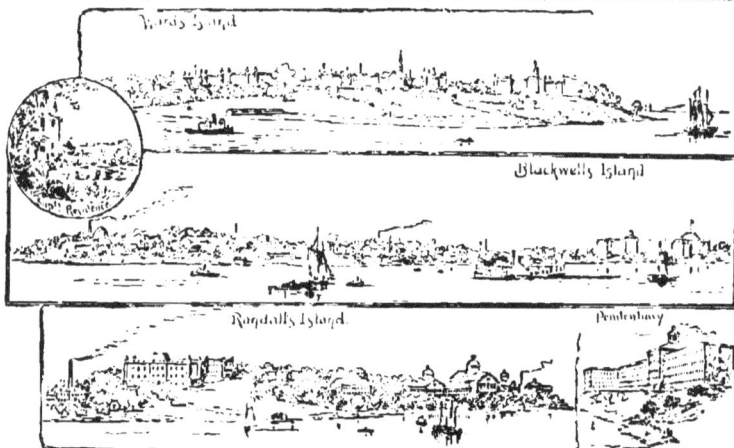

the East River, all of which are used for charitable and correctional institutions.

Grand Island (8), North Hero Island (9), and Isle La Motte (10) belong to Vermont, but Lake Champlain contains within New York

territory a multitude of small islands like that shown in this picture, which are used for summer residences.

Of the group of 1800 islands known as The Thousand Islands a good many belong to New York, among which the best known are Wells, or Wellesly Island (10), on which are Thousand Island and Westminster Parks; and Grindstone Island (15).

Wolfe Island (12), and Prince Edward Island (13) belong to Canada. Carleton Island, off the southeast of Wolfe Island, belongs to New York. Durham's "Carleton Island in the Revolution" tells much of interest in its history. Of the islands at the foot of Lake Ontario, Duck Island belongs to Canada, and Grenadier, Galloo, and Stony Islands to New York, the boundary line being equi-distant from the two shores.

The Thousand Islands have figured much in song and story, as Hough in his "Thousand Islands" has shown. Cooper's "The Pathfinder" gives vivid descriptions of this region. Charles Dickens in his "American Notes" says:

We left Kingston for Montreal on the 10th of May, at half-past nine in the morning, and proceeded in a steamboat down the St. Lawrence River. The beauty of this noble stream at almost any point, but especially in the commencement of this journey, where it winds its way among the Thousand Islands, can hardly be imagined. The number and constant succession of these Islands, all green and richly wooded; their fluctuating sizes, so large, that for half an hour together, one among them will appear as the opposite bank of the river, and some so small that they are mere dimples on its bosom,—their infinite variety of shapes,—and the numberless combinations of beautiful forms which the trees growing on them present;—all form a picture fraught with uncommon interest and pleasure.

Lossing's 'Field Book of the Revolution" says:

We passed the morning in alternately viewing the ever-changing scene as our vessel sped towards Ontario, and in perusing Burke's "Essay on the Sublime and Beautiful". I never read that charming production with so much pleasure as then, for illustrative examples were on every side. And when, towards noon, our course was among the Thousand Islands, the propriety of the stars as an example, by their number and confusion, of the cause of the idea of sublimity, was forcibly illustrated. "The apparent disorder," he says, augments the grandeur, for the appearance of care is highly contrary to our idea of magnificence." So with these islands. They fill the St. Lawrence through nearly 60 miles of its course, commencing 15 miles below Kingston, and varying in size from a few yards to 18 miles in length. Some are mere syenitic rocks, bearing sufficient alluvium to produce cedar, spruce, and pine shrubs, which seldom grow to the dignity of a tree; while others were beautifully fringed with luxuriant grass and shaded by lofty trees. A few of the larger are inhabited and cultivated. They are 1,227 in number. Viewed separately, they present nothing remarkable; but scattered, as they are, so profusely and in such disorder over the bosom of the river, their features constantly changing as we made our rapid way among them, an idea of magnificence and sublimity involuntarily possessed the mind, and wooed our attention from the tuition of books to that of nature.

Grand Island (14) forms, with Buckhorn and Beaver Islands, close by, a township of Erie county. It contains 18,500 acres.

Navy Island, is shown in the map, below Grand Island. Just above Niagara Falls is Goat Island, half a mile long, well shown in the picture on page 22.

IV. GEOLOGY

While this topic can be only touched upon in a book like this, it has an important connection with the geography of New York from the fact that this State has given to modern geology much of its nomenclature, because a long line of geological strata are better shown here than elsewhere.

The following rough outlines show the greater geological divisions of the State as laid down by Dr. Hall in his geological map of 1842.

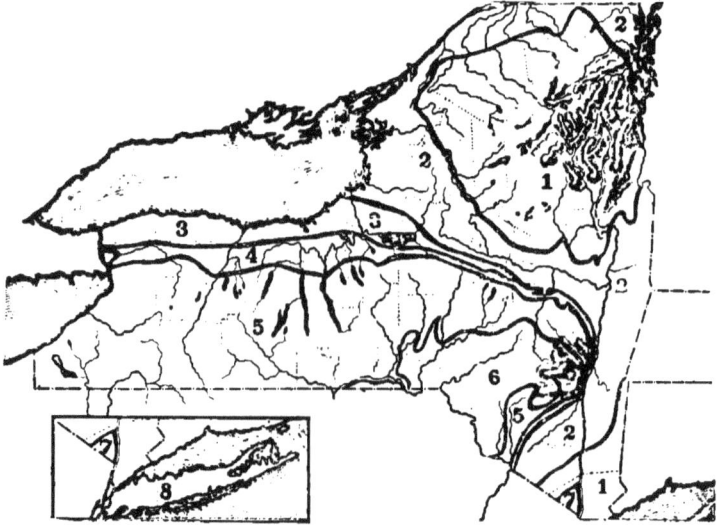

A new map is now under way. In Dana's "Geological Story Briefly Told" the geological strata are named as follows :

			American.	British.
Cenozoic	B. Quaternary		c. Recent. b. Champlain*. a. Glacial.	The same. " " " "
	A. Tertiary		c. Pliocene. b. Miocene. a. Eocene.	" " " " " "
Mezozoic	(Reptiles)		c. Cretaceous. b. Jurassic. a. Triassic.	" " " " " "
Paleozoic	C. Carboniferous (Coal-plants)		c. Permian b. Carboniferous a. Subcarbonifous.	" " " " Mountain limestone.
	B. Devonian (Fishes)		d. Catskill*. c. Portage* and Chemung*. b. Hamilton* a. { Upper Helderberg*. { Corniferous.	} Old red sandstone.
	A. Silurian (Invertebrates)	Upper	a. Oriskany.* c. Lower Helderberg*. b. Salina*. a. Niagara*.	} Ludlow group. } Wenlock group.
		Lower	c. Trenton*. Llandeilo. b. Canadian. Tremadoc. a. Primordial. Cambrian.	
Archean.				

The names starred are all New York names, taken from places where these rocks are best shown.

Dr. Hall's own classification of the rocks is as follows, and the numbers in heavy type are those given on the map.

(8) VIII. Quaternary.
   VII. Tertiary.
(7) VI. New red sandstone.
   V. Carboniferous system.
(6) IV. Old red sandstone.

(5) D. Erie Division.
- 28. Chemung group.
  - c. Cashaqua shale.
  - b. Gardeau flagstones.
  - a. Portage sandstone.
- 27. Portage or Nunda group
- 26. Genesee slate.
- 25. Tully limestone
  - c. Ludlowville shales.
  - b. Encrinal shales.
  - a. Moscow shales.
- 24. Hamilton group.
- 23. Marcellus slate.

} Devonian system.

(4) C. Helderberg series.
- 22. Corniferous limestone.
- 21. Onondaga limestone.
- 20. Scholarie grit.
- 19. Cauda-galli grit.
- 18. Oriskany sandstone.
- 17. Upper Pentamerus limestone.
- 16. Encrinal limestone.
- 15. Delthyris shaly limestone.
- 14. Pentamerus limestone.
- 13. Waterlime group.
- 12. Onondaga salt group.

} Silurian system.

(3) B. Ontario division.
- 11. Niagara group.
- 10. Clinton group.
- 9. Medina sandstone.

(2) A. Champlain division.
- 8. Oneida conglomerate.
- 7. Grey sandstone.
- 6. Hudson river group.
- 5. Utica slate.
- 4. Trenton limestone.
  - b. Birdseye.
  - a. Chazy.
- 3. Black river limestone.
- 2. Calciferous sandrock.
- 1. Potsdam sandstone.

} Cambrian system.

(1) Primary or Hypogene.

The following view of the strata as they lie across the State is taken from his Geology of the Fourth District.

A. Primary.
B. Potsdam sandstone.
C. Calciferous sandrock.
D. Black-river limestone.
E. Trenton limestone.
F. Utica slate.
G. Hudson-river group.
H. Grey sandstone and Oneida conglomerate.
I. Medina sandstone.
K. Clinton group.
L. l. Niagara group.
M. Onondaga-salt group.
N. Helderberg series.
O. Hamilton group, including Marcellus and Moscow shale.
e. Tully limestone.
P. Portage group and Genesee slate.
R. Chemung group.
S. Old Red system.
T. Conglomerate of the Carboniferous system.
a. Lake Ontario.

The distance upon the N. side of the lake has been much shortened in proportion, in order to give more room for the rocks upon the s. side.

From the absence of all extensive disturbances of the strata, we are enabled to trace an uninterrupted series from the Potsdam sandstone to the Old Red. No where is there known to exist so complete a series of the older fossiliferous rocks as those embraced within the limits of our State, and terminating at a point of great and important change in the condition of the surface, and included between this and the rocks of metamorphic origin, we have here offered one of the most decided and best characterized systems known in the whole world.—*Hall, Geology of Fourth District, p. 20.*

The geological formation of the State makes its quarries valuable. By the census of 1890 it stands 3d of the States in the value of its entire stone product ($84,418,143), ranking 1st of the States in the value of its bluestone ($1,363,321), millstones, and graphite ; 2d in gypsum ; 3d in marble ; 4th in slate ; 5th in limestone and sandstone ; 18th in granite.

Roofing-slate is quarried in Washington, Rensselaer, and Columbia counties ; sandstone at Potsdam and at Medina; flagstones in the region of Kingston ; white marble in Westchester county, black marble at Glens Falls, red marble at Warwick, and verd-antique at Moriah ; tale in St. Lawrence county ; gypsum near Syracuse ; hydraulic cement at Rondout, Manlius, and Akron.

It has no coal, but is ranked 2d in the value of its iron product ($3,100,216). The petroleum wells of the Allegany and Cataraugus district, of 31 square miles (see page 56), are included by the census in the Bradford district, the product of which for 1889 was 7,158,363 bbls. Of natural gas the Allegany county wells in 1889 produced 1330 million feet, and the value of that consumed in New York was $204,325.

In the value of mineral waters produced in 1889 New York stands 3d ($239,975), Wisconsin standing 1st, California 2d, and Virginia 4th. The salt product has been spoken of (page 56).

V. CLIMATE AND PRODUCTIONS

CLIMATE

The climate of New York is remarkably varied. While Long Island and its vicinity has, owing to the influence of the ocean, a comparatively even temperature, seldom reaching zero or rising above 95°, in the State at large the usual range is from −20° to 100°, giving a variety that is stimulating and not disagreeable to people of a sound constitution.

Frosts begin from September 1st to October 1st, and end from April 1st to May 1st, according to the locality and year. In the Adirondack region the snow-fall is heavy, the winter long and severe. In central New York it is not uncommon for snow to accumulate to the depth of 3 or 4 feet, and yet this is not persistent. About New York city and on Long Island the snow rarely exceeds a foot in depth, sleighing is always uncertain, and sometimes the ground will be bare for weeks together. Thus it will be seen that the climate of New York is intermediate in character between that of New England and that of the Mississippi valley States,—a little milder than the former, severer than the latter. The great lakes which border it are never frozen to their centres, and exert an equalizing influence upon the climate of their shores.

The local variation of climate within the limits of the State will be best seen by the following table :—

	Lat.	Long.	Elevation.	Mean Annual Temp.	Mean Annual Rainfall.
	° ′	° ′	Feet.	°	Inches.
Moriches, Long Island	40 49	72 36	Sea-level.	54.2	54.67
New York City	40 42	74	100	51.2	44.59
Albany	42 40	74 45	150	46.9	40.67
Rochester	43 8	77 51	525	46.9	32.56
Buffalo	42 53	78 55	660	46.8	33.84
Gouverneur	44 25	75 35	400	44.1	30.15
Plattsburgh	44 41	73 25	186	44	33.4

PLANTS AND TREES

Originally the surface of New York was occupied by an almost unbroken forest, and, as a consequence of the general fertility of the soil, its topographical diversity, and the range of latitude and longitude, the flora is rich and varied. About 70 species of trees are known to inhabit the State, and these include all found in the adjacent portions of the Union and Canada.

The most abundant are oaks, of which there are 15 species ; but with these mingle 5 species each of maple, pine, and poplar, 4 species of hickory, 3 each of elm, spruce, and ash, 2 of willow, cherry, magnolia, and pepperidge, and 1 each of larch, liriodendron, dogwood, arbor vitæ, balsam, yew, sycamore, honey locust, sweet gum, locust, butternut, black walnut, chestnut, beech, hornbeam, basswood, sassafras, and mulberry.

On the summits of the Adirondacks a true alpine vegetation is found, though consisting of but a small number of plants ; several of these exist in no other locality in the United States except the mountain summits of Vermont and New Hampshire. The flowering plants and ferns of New York were studied with much care by the late Dr. Torrey, and his report upon them forms two quarto volumes of the *Report on the Natural History of New York*. The flowering plants enumerated by Dr. Torrey amount to 1540 species, to which a few additions have since been made. The ferns number 54 species —more than are found in any other State ; the lower forms of plant life, seaweeds, fungi, lichens, etc., are constantly supplying new material, and many years will yet be required for their complete elaboration.

ANIMALS

At the advent of the whites the fauna of New York included all the wild animals which were found in the north-eastern States of the Union or the adjacent portions of Canada, but by the cutting off of forests, and the occupation of the surface by farms, the range of the native animals has been greatly reduced, and they have been unceasingly destroyed by man.

Formerly the elk, the moose, and the caribou were abundant in the N. part of the State, but are now all exterminated, while the Virginia deer in many localities is still quite plentiful. Of the carnivorous animals, the couguar, the black bear, two species of lynx, the red and grey foxes, the wolf, otter, fisher, pine marten, mink, and skunk still remain, but the wolf is on the eve of extermination, and the wolverine, never abundant, has perhaps migrated northward. Among the rodents the beaver and variable hare are found, but in small numbers, while rabbits, squirrels, rats, mice, field-mice, etc., are still unpleasantly numerous.

Civilization has made but little difference with the reptiles, birds and fishes. All the birds indigenous to the E. portion of the continent may probably at times be found within the State, though their relative numbers are affected by the removal of the forests.

Among the reptiles are 17 species of snakes, 3 of which, two rattlesnakes and the copperhead, are venomous. The fishes include all the species found in the lower lakes, in the rivers of the temperate portions of the continent, and on the Atlantic coast ; and the fisheries constitute an important element in the revenues and subsistence of the people. The streams and lakes of the more elevated portions contain brook trout in abundance ; those of the lower levels are well stocked with bass, pickerel, perch, and other fish.

VI. POLITICAL DIVISIONS

COUNTIES

New York is divided into 60 counties as shown on the map upon the following page. Their origin and other interesting facts are given in the following table:

No. on Map.	Name.	Date of Erection.	Formed from what.	Origin of name.	County Seat	Population, 1890.
31	Albany.	1683	Original.	Duke of York.	Albany,	164,555
2	Allegany.	1806	Genesee.	Allegany river.	Belmont.	43,240
16	Broome.	1806	Tioga.	John Broome.	Binghamton.	62,973
21	Cattaraugus.	1808	Genesee.	Indian name.	Little Valley.	60,866
45	Cayuga.	1799	Onondaga.	Indian tribe.	Auburn.	65,302
22	Chautauqua.	1808	Genesee.	Indian name.	Mayville.	75,202
18	Chemung.	1836	Tioga.	Chemung river.	Elmira.	48,265
31	Chenango.	1798	Herkimer and Tioga.	Chenango river.	Norwich.	37,776
54	Clinton.	1788	Washington.	George Clinton.	Plattsburgh.	46,437
13	Columbia.	1786	Albany.	Columbus.	Hudson.	46,172
30	Cortland.	1808	Onondaga.	Pierre Van Cortlandt	Cortland.	28,657
15	Delaware.	1797	Ulster and Otsego.	Delaware river.	Delhi.	45,496
10	Dutchess.	1683	Original.	Duchess of York.	Poughkeepsie.	77,879
23	Erie.	1821	Niagara.	Lake Erie.	Buffalo.	322,981
57	Essex.	1799	Clinton.	County of England.	Elizabethtown.	33,052
59	Franklin.	1808	Clinton.	Benjamin Franklin.	Malone.	38,110
33	Fulton.	1838	Montgomery.	Robert Fulton.	Johnstown.	37,650
47	Genesee.	1802	Ontario.	Genesee river.	Batavia.	33,265
11	Greene.	1800	Albany and Ulster.	Nathaniel Greene.	Catskill.	31,598
55	Hamilton.	1816	Montgomery.	Alexander Hamilton	Sageville.	4,762
41	Herkimer.	1791	Montgomery.	Nicholas Herkimer.	Herkimer.	45,608
53	Jefferson.	1805	Oneida.	Thomas Jefferson.	Watertown.	68,806
3	Kings.	1683	Original.	King Charles II.	Brooklyn.	838,547
54	Lewis.	1805	Oneida.	Morgan Lewis.	Lowville.	29,806
25	Livingston	1821	Genesee and Ontario.	Robert R. Livingston	Geneseo.	37,801
44	Madison.	1806	Chenango.	James Madison.	Morrisville.	42,892
50	Monroe.	1821	Ontario and Geneseo.	James Monroe.	Rochester.	189,586
40	Montgomery*	1772	Albany.	Richard Montgomery	Fonda.	45,699
5	New York.	1683	Original.	City and county iden	tical.	1,515,301
48	Niagara.	1808	Genesee.	Niagara river.	Lockport.	62,491
42	Oneida.	1798	Herkimer.	Indian tribe.	Utica.	122,922
44	Onondaga.	1794	Herkimer.	Indian tribe.	Syracuse.	146,247
46	Ontario.	1789	Montgomery.	Lake Ontario.	Canandaigua.	48,453
8	Orange.	1683	Original.	Son of Duke of York	Goshen, Newburgh.	97,859
49	Orleans.	1821	Genesee.		Albion.	30,803
52	Oswego.	1816	Oneida and Onondaga.	City of Oswego.	Pulaski, Oswego.	71,883
32	Otsego.	1791	Montgomery.	Indian name.	Cooperstown.	50,861
9	Putnam.	1812	Dutchess.	Israel Putnam.	Carmel.	14,849
2	Queens.	1683	Original.	Wife of Charles II.	Jamaica.	128,059
36	Rensselaer.	1791	Albany.	Van Rensselaer family.	Troy.	124,511
4	Richmond.	1683	Original.	Son of Charles II.	Richmond.	51,693
7	Rockland.	1798	Orange.	Descriptive.	Clarkstown.	35,162
60	St. Lawrence.	1802	Clinton, Montgomery and Herkimer.	St. Lawrence river.	Canton.	85,048
38	Saratoga.	1791	Albany.	Indian name.	Ballston Spa.	57,663
35	Schenectady.	1809	Albany.	Indian name.	Schenectady.	29,797
34	Schoharie.	1795	Albany and Otsego.	Indian name.	Schoharie.	29,164
28	Schuyler.	1854	Steuben, Chemung and Tompkins.	Philip Schuyler	Watkins.	16,711
27	Seneca.	1804	Cayuga.	Indian tribe.	Ovid, Waterloo.	28,227
19	Steuben.	1796	Ontario.	Baron Steuben.	Bath.	81,473
1	Suffolk.	1683	Original.	County of England.	Riverhead.	62,491
12	Sullivan.	1809	Ulster.	John Sullivan.	Monticello.	31,031
17	Tioga.	1791	Montgomery.	Indian name.	Owego.	29,935
29	Tompkins.	1817	Cayuga and Seneca.	Daniel D. Tompkins.	Ithaca.	32,923
11	Ulster.	1683	Original.	Irish Earldom of Duke of York.	Kingston.	87,062
56	Warren.	1813	Washington.	Joseph Warren.	Caldwell.	27,866
37	Washington.†	1772	Albany.	George Washington.	Argyle.	45,690
51	Wayne.	1823	Ontario and Seneca	Anthony Wayne.	Lyons.	49,729
6	Westchester.	1683	Original.	Town of Westchester	White Plains.	146,772
21	Wyoming.	1841	Genesee.		Warsaw.	31,193
26	Yates.	1823	Ontario.	Joseph C. Yates.	Penn Yan.	21,001

* Changed from Tryon, 1784.   † Changed from Charlotte, 1784.   Total, 5,997,853

COUNTIES

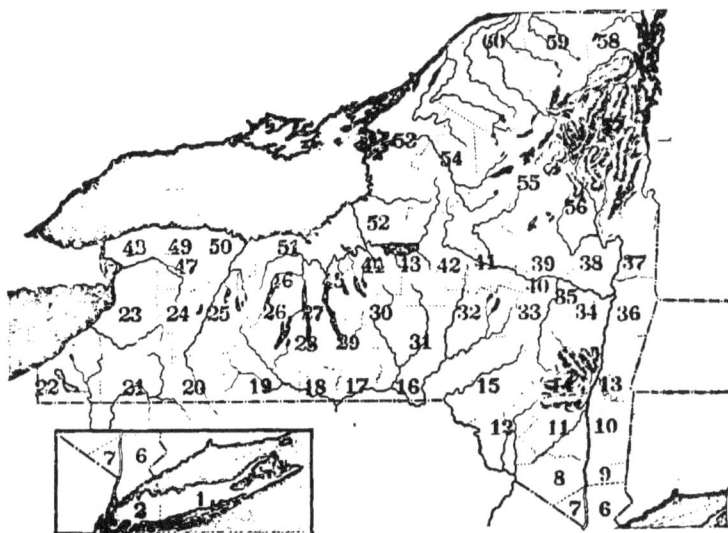

INDIAN RESERVATIONS

Part of the territory of the State is still occupied by Indians, who hold, as separate nations, reservations as follows:

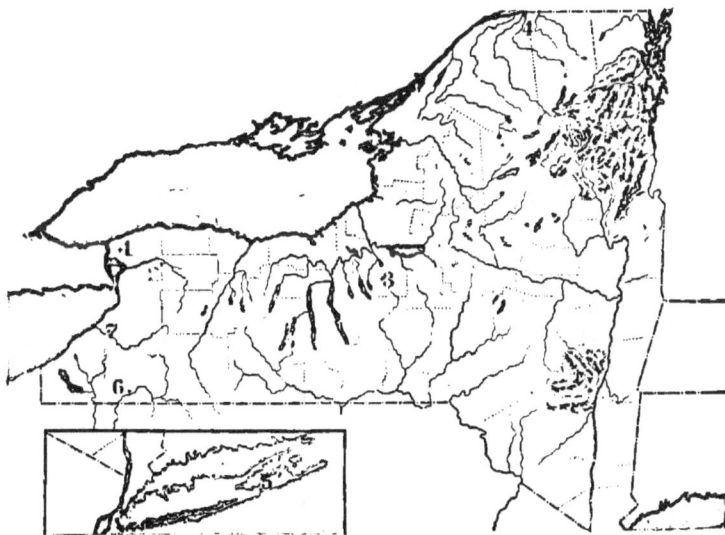

7. Allegany,
6. Cattaraugus,
3. Onondaga,
4. St. Regis,

5. Shinnecock,
2. Tonawanda,
1. Tuscarora.

The Indians of New York number about 5,000 and occupy lands covering 87,677 acres on the following reservations: Tuscarora (1); Tonawanda (2); Onondaga (3); St. Regis (4); Shinnecock (5); Allegany (6) and Cattaraugus (7), the last two being occupied by the Senecas. The presiding officer of the general league has always been chosen from the Onondagas. Schools are conducted upon these reservations under direction of the Superintendent of Public Instruction.

A remnant of the Oneida indians, numbering 175, reside at Orchard Park, Oneida county, and Windfall, Madison county. There are a few Poosepatucks near Brook haven, Suffolk County, and some 8 or 10 Montauks, at Montauk Point.

The Allegany reservation is 40 miles long, on both sides of the Allegany River, from the Pennsylvania line, and covers 30,469 acres. The Cattaraugus reservation extends some 42 miles from Lake Erie up Cattaraugus Creek, and covers 21,680 acres.

Full information as to these reservations may be found in the "Report of the Special Committee to investigate the Indian Problem of the State of New York", 8\282, Albany, 1888.

CITIES

The following map shows the cities of the State.

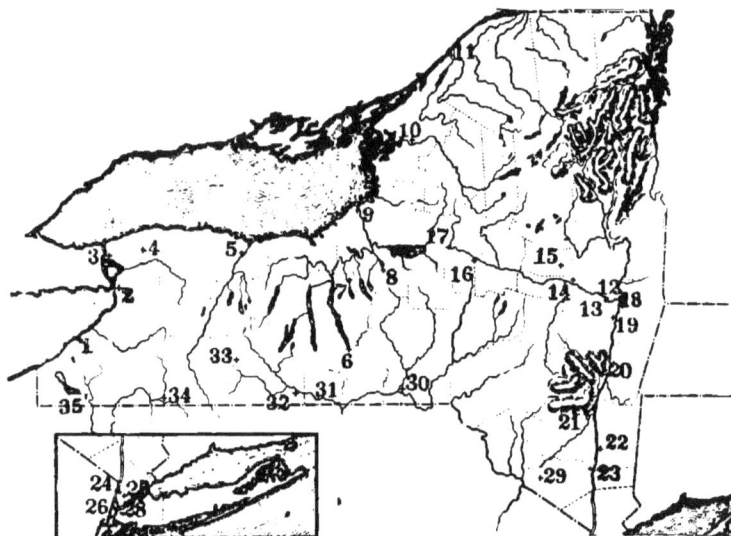

They are placed in order of population, and numbered as upon the map. The classification is according to the Constitution.

	Date of Incorpor'n	Pop'n in 1860	Pop'n in 1870	Pop'n in 1880	Pop'n in 1890	State Cen. 1892	Pages where referred to in this book
First Class							
26. New York,	1680	805,658	942,292	1,206,299	1,515,301	1,801,739	11, 61, 66, 68, 74-77, 83, 85, 91, 92, 107, 113, 117
27. Brooklyn,	1834	266,661	396,099	566,663	806,343	930,633	60, 66, 68, 74, 92, 117
2. Buffalo,	1832	81,129	117,714	155,134	255,664	278,796	11, 12, 43, 66, 68, 74-77, 79, 97, 109-111, 116, 117
Second Class							
5. Rochester,	1834	48,204	62,386	89,366	133,896	144,834	25, 33, 43, 66, 68, 74, 76, 78, 96, 98, 110, 111, 116, 117

19. Albany,	1686...	62.367..	69,422...	90.758..	94.923..	97.12C..11, 42, 43, 66, 68, 75, 77, 83, 84, 86, 105, 114	
8. Syracuse,	1847...	28.119...	43.051...	51.792...	88.143...	91.941..11, 43, 56, 66, 68, 74, 76, 80, 81, 83, 99, 107, 109, 113	
18. Troy,	1816...	39.235...	46,105...	56.747...	60,956...	64,986..27, 29, 68, 74, 85, 104, 105, 111	

Third Class.

16. Utica.	1832...	22.529...	28,804...	33.914...	44,007...	46,608..43, 64, 76, 81, 82, 83, 99, 107, 108, 113
28. L. I. City,	1870...			17.129...	30.506...	35.745..60, 62, 117
30. Binghamton.	1867...	8.325...	12,692...	17.317...	35.005...	34.514..11, 68, 76, 96, 101, 107
24. Yonkers,	1872...	11.848...	18.357...	18.892...	32.833...	31.419..91
31. Elmira.	1864...	8.082...	15.863...	20.541...	30.893...	29.911..11, 68, 74, 76, 96, 109, 110, 116
7. Auburn,	1848...	10.986...	17.225...	21.924...	25.858...	24.737..68, 76, 79, 81, 110
23. Newburgh,	1865...		17.014...	18.049...	23.087...	24.536..28, 68, 89, 93
12. Cohoes,	1869...	8.800..	15.357...	19.416...	22.509...	23.231..27, 44, 85, 105
22. Poughkeepsie.	1854...	14,726...	20,080...	20.207...	22.206...	23.196..68, 74, 76, 87, 89
13. Schenectady,	1798...		11.026...	13.655...	19.902...	22.858..43, 68, 74, 85, 103
9. Oswego,	1848...	16.816...	20.910...	21.116..	21.842...	21.966..15, 25, 33, 43, 57, 68, 75, 98, 107, 113
21. Kingston.	1872...			18.344...	21.261...	21.495..66, 68, 95, 114, 116
33. Jamestown,	1886...		5.336...	9.357...	16.038...	18.617..97, 98
14. Amsterdam,	1885...		5.426...	9.466...	17.336...	18.242..85
10. Watertown,	1869...	7.567..	9.336...	10.697...	14.725...	16.982..49, 68, 93, 99
4. Lockport.	1865...		12.426...	13.522...	16.038...	16.088..42, 68, 78, 79, 97
15. Gloversville,	1890...		4.518...	7.133..	13.864...	14.694..83
25. Mt. Vernon,	1892...					14.000..114
6. Ithaca,	1888...		8.462...	9.105...	11.079 ..	13.450..47, 48, 68. 74, 109, 110, 116
17. Rome,	1870...	9.289...	11.000...	12.194...	14.991...	13.038..15, 42, 44, 76. 81. 82, 99, 100, 113
11. Ogdensburg,	1868...4	7.409..	10.076...	10.311...	11.662...	11.955..76. 99
34. Olean.	1894...				11.507...	........97, 111
33. Hornellsville,	1888...		4.552 ..	8.195...	10.996...	11.898..97, 111
3. Niagara Falls	1892...					11.711..11, 22. 74, 78 79, 97, 98, 100
29. Middletown,	1888...		6.049...	8.494...	11.977...	11.612..76, 92, 93, 113
1. Dunkirk,	1880...			7.248...	9.416...	10.040..93, 97, 111, 117
32. Corning,	1890...		4.018...	4.802...	8.550...	10.025..96, 109, 117
20. Hudson,	1785...		8.615...	8.670...	9.970...	9.642..57, 68, 76, 85, 114

In manufacturing, the statistics of the larger cities are given as follows in the census of 1890. They are numbered according to the amounts.

7. Albany	$ 25,536,486	16. Newburgh	$ 6,964,287
13. Auburn	9,634,785	1. New York	777,322,721
11. Binghamton	15,040,152	15. Oswego	7,482,378
2. Brooklyn	269,244,147	17. Poughkeepsie	6,254,132
3. Buffalo	100,052,208	4. Rochester	65,091,156
12. Cohoes	10,836,260	5. Syracuse	29,297,241
14. Elmira	8,844,936	6. Troy	29,248,750
18. Kingston	4,009,574	10. Utica	15,615,715
9. Long Island City	16,200,226	8. Yonkers	21,319,017

It has been thought best to treat of the cities and villages as the traveller along our lines of railway would come to them, on pages 77 to 118. But those who prefer to study them topically may do so intelligently by looking up the references given and comparing the statistics in these tables.

Thus Elmira is 146 miles from Buffalo (see page 11), the county seat of Chemung County (68), the seat of Elmira College (74) and of a Reformatory (76), and on the Erie (96), D. L. & W. (109), Lehigh Valley (110), E. C. & N., and Pa. (116) railways, etc.

The following villages of the State had more than 4,000 population under the census of 1890. They are arranged in the order of popula-

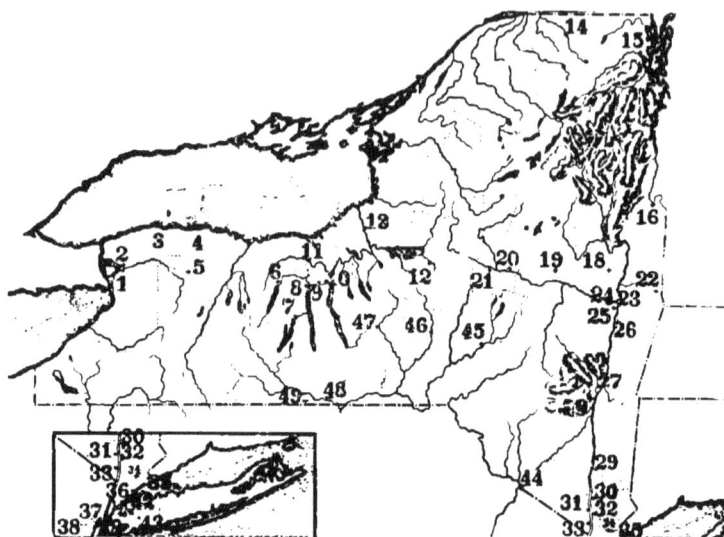

tion, and numbered as on the map. Owego is placed last because no separate returns were made in the enumeration. There are other villages which have more than 4,000 population which are not given here because not officially enumerated separately. The figures following give pages where the village is referred to in this book.

37. New Brighton,
39. Edgewater (Stapleton)
25. West Troy, 43, 105
18. Saratoga Springs, 11, 57, 85, 103
23. Lansingburg
30. Peekskill, 90
17. Glens Falls, 40, 44, 57, 66, 72, 103
32. Sing Sing, 76, 91
44. Port Jervis, 30, 92, 93
20. Little Falls, 15, 19, 27, 57, 58, 72, 83
47. Cortland, 68, 75, 109, 116
41. Flushing, 60, 118
36. New Rochelle, 114
19. Johnstown, 68, 83
8. Geneva, 43, 74, 79, 81, 110, 117
26. Greenbush

5. Batavia, 68, 76, 78, 97, 110
1. Tonawanda, 43, 77, 79, 97
22. Hoosick Falls, 85
15. Plattsburgh, 66, 68, 75, 100, 101
39. Port Richmond
15. Oneonta, 75, 106, 107
40. College Point, 118
10. Seneca Falls, 48, 81
12. Oneida, 81, 113
6. Canandaigua, 68, 78, 79, 81
42. Jamaica, 60, 68, 75, 118
35. Port Chester, 114
46. Norwich, 68, 109, 113
31. Haverstraw, 91
44. Malone, 68, 76, 100
27. Catskill, 68, 85

43. Hempstead, 60, 118
2. North Tonawanda, 43, 77, 79, 97
4. Albion, 68, 78, 79
3. Medina, 17, 66, 78, 79
11. Lyons, 43, 68, 79, 117
24. Green Island, 105
16. Whitehall, 11, 42, 44, 103
9. Waterloo, 68, 81
29. Matteawan, 89
7. Penn Yan, 57, 68, 116, 117
28. Saugerties
13. Fulton, 25, 48, 99, 109, 113
49. Waverly, 96, 109
33. Nyack, 91, 92, 93
21. Ilion, 83
34. White Plains, 68, 114
48. Owego, 68, 96, 109, 110

VII. EDUCATION

The system of education in New York is peculiar in that it is under double control. The Department of Public Instruction has charge of all schools supported by public tax, while the University of the State of New York, usually called the Regents, from the name of its officers, has control of secondary and higher education, both in public and in private institutions.

The Department of Public Instruction is administered by a Superintendent, elected by the Legislature for three years at a salary of $5,000 a year. He appoints the subordinates in his office, including the institute instructors and the inspectors of teachers' classes ; and he confirms the election by the local boards of the teachers in normal schools. His authority is broader than is entrusted to this officer in any other State. His decisions on school matters are not subject to reversal by the courts. The portrait

CHARLES R. SKINNER

of the present Superintendent is here given.

Next to him in authority are the School Commissioners, who have local supervision of all the schools of the State except in cities and villages which employ Superintendents. These Commissioners and Superintendents report to the State Superintendent.

Next come the Trustees of district schools, and the Boards of Education of union schools, who have immediate charge of their schools, receiving and expending the money raised, employing teachers, making regulations, etc.

The University of the State of New York, usually referred to as the Regents, from the name of its board of control, has in charge the incorporation of higher institutions of learning, the granting of degrees, the distribution of certain funds on the basis of examination, and hence the establishing of courses of study for secondary schools, the care of the State Library, State Museum, etc. Its executive officer is the Secretary, who is also the State Librarian.

The State Library, in the Capitol of Albany is the headquarters of a Library School which sends out librarians to libraries all over the country. Its own equipment is remarkably complete, and every facility is granted for the use of books by authors and others either there or anywhere in the State.

For full particulars as to the school law of the State, see Bardeen's "Handbook for School Trustees".

For a full account of the Civil Government of the State, see Northam's "Civil Government for Common Schools".

The following map shows the location of the colleges of the State.

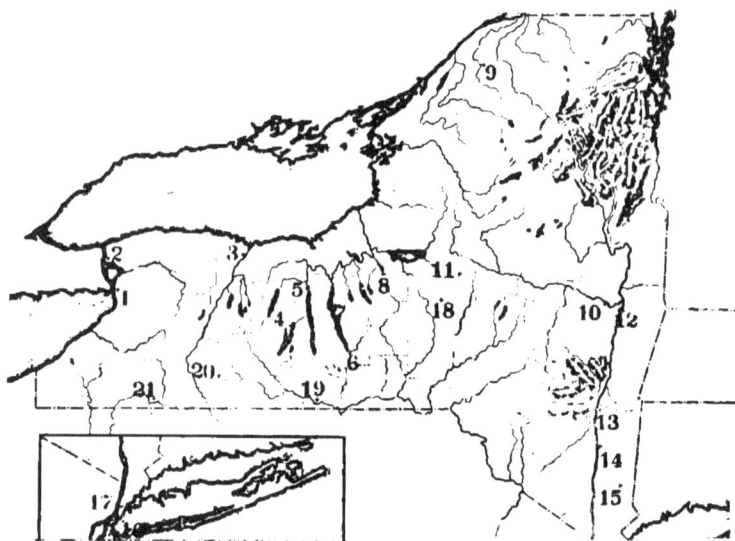

The number prefixed shows the location on the map, the date is that of incorporation, and the next number gives reference to page.

20. Alfred University, Alfred Centre, 1857.

17. Barnard College, New York, 1889. 91

1. Canisius College, Buffalo, 1883. 78

18. Colgate University, Hamilton, 1846. 113

17. College of St. Francis Xavier, New York, 1861. 91

17. College of the City of New York, 1854. 91

17. Columbia College, New York, 1754. 91

6. Cornell University, Ithaca, 1865. 55 48. 109

15. Drew Female College, Carmel, 1866. 114

19. Elmira College, Elmira, 1855. 96

11. Hamilton College, Clinton, 1812. 113

5. Hobart College, Geneva, 1825. 81

4. Keuka College, Keuka College, 1892. 57

17. Manhattan College, New York, 1863. 91

2. Niagara University, Niagara Falls, 1883. 78

17. Normal College of the City of New York, 1888. 91

16. Polytechnic Institute of Brooklyn, 1869. 60

12. Rensselaer Polytechnic Institute, Troy, 1824. 105

17. Rutgers Female College, New York 1867. 91

21. St. Bonaventure's College, Allegany, 1875. 74

16. St. Francis's College, Brooklyn, 1884. 60

16. St John's College, Brooklyn, 1871. 60

17. St. John's College, Fordham, 1846. 91

9. St. Lawrence University, Canton, 1856. 100

13. St. Stephen's College, Anandale, 1860. 74

8. Syracuse University, Syracuse, 1870. 81

17. Teachers' College, New York, 1887. 91

10. Union College, Schenectady, 1795. 85

17. University of the City of New York, 1831. 91

3. University of Rochester, Rochester, 1851. 78

14. Vassar College, Poughkeepsie, 1861. 89

7. Wells College, Aurora 1868. 110

NORMAL SCHOOLS

The following map shows the location of the Normal Schools.   The

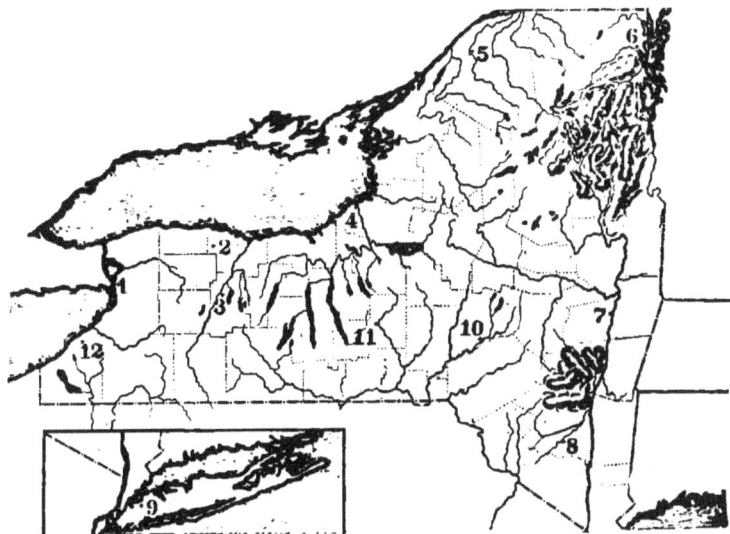

numbers following the name give the pages on which the principal reference is made in this book to the places where they are located.

7. Albany Normal College. 85	9. Jamaica. 60, 118
2. Brockport. 79	8. New Paltz. 89, 116
1. Buffalo. 78	10. Oneonta. 107
11. Cortland. 109	4. Oswego. 99
12. Fredonia. 59, 98	6. Plattsburgh. 101
3. Genesco. 68	5. Potsdam. 100.

The Normal College and the Teachers' College of New York City are not State institutions, and are named on page 74 among the colleges.

Besides its Normal Schools, New York has an extensive system of educating teachers through Teachers' Institutes and Training Classes.   An institute of one week is held at least once every year in every Commissioner District in the State, and all teachers are required to attend, except those in cities and in villages of at least 5,000 inhabitants.   Instruction is free, and is given by a corps of teachers appointed by the State Superintendent.

Training Classes are held in Academies and Union Schools designated by the State Superintendent.   Tuition is free to the members of the classes, but is paid for by the State at the rate of one dollar a week for each student.   On completion of the work students who pass the required examination receive a special second-grade certificate.

A. S. DOWNING

Both Teachers' Institutes and Training Classes are under special direction of a Supervisor, appointed by the State Superintendent.   The portrait of the present Supervisor is given above.

CHARITABLE AND CORRECTIONAL INSTITUTIONS

New York is very liberal in her provisions for the unfortunate and the criminal classes. The principal institutions are located as shown on the following map. New York city is not numbered. The num-

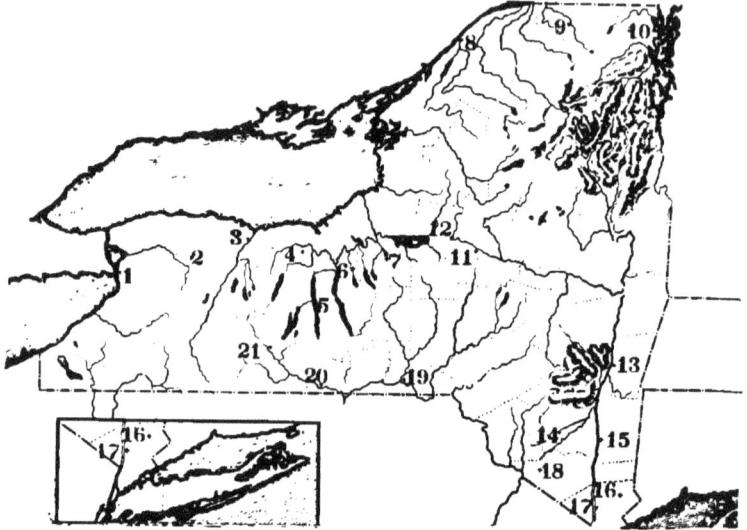

bers following the names give the pages of this book on which the principal reference is made to the places in which the institutions are located.

PRISONS
6. Auburn. 81
10. Dannemora. 100
15. Sing Sing. 91

REFORMATORIES
For Boys and Men
20. Elmira. 96
14. Napanock.
    New York (House of Refuge). 91
3. Rochester Industrial School. 78
For Women
16. Bedford Station. 114
13. House of Refuge, Hudson. 85

INSTITUTIONS FOR THE BLIND
2. Batavia. 78
    New York. 91

INSTITUTIONS FOR DEAF-MUTES
1. Buffalo. 77
    Fordham (New York). 91
9. Malone. 100
    New York. 91

3. Rochester. 78
12. Rome. 81

ASYLUMS FOR THE FEEBLE-MINDED
7. Syracuse. 81
4. Custodial Asylum for Women, Newark. 116

ASYLUMS FOR THE INSANE
6. Auburn (Insane Criminals). 81
    Matteawan (Insane Criminals).
19. Binghamton. 96
1. Buffalo. 77
18. Middletown (Homeopathic). 93
8. Ogdensburg. 100
5. Ovid (Willard Asylum). 110
15. Poughkeepsie. 89
3. Rochester. 78
11. Utica. 83

MISCELLANEOUS
19. Asylum for Inebriates, Binghamton. 96
21. Soldiers' and Sailors' Home, Bath. 96
11. Masonic Home, Utica. 83

VIII. RAILWAY JOURNEYS THROUGH THE STATE

1. The New York Central and Hudson River R.R.

This railway is advertised, not without reason, as " America's greatest railroad ".   In its length, its equipment, the number and speed and comfort of its trains, it is probably unequalled anywhere.   Its main

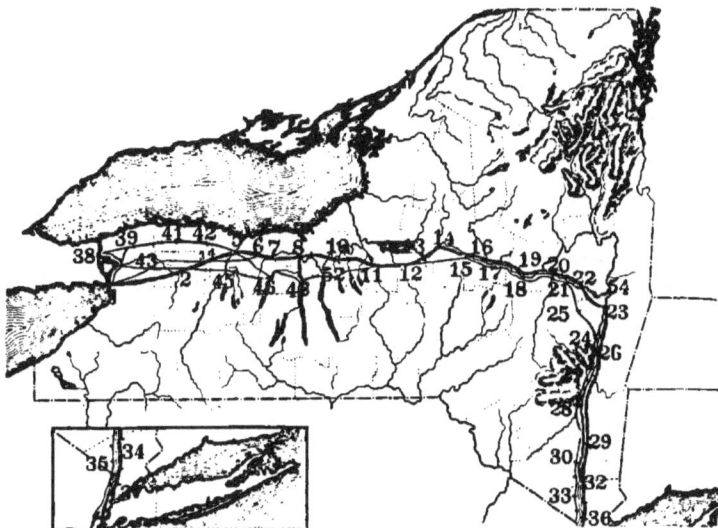

line reaches from Buffalo to New York city, 440 miles, and its branches cover much of the State with network.   From Buffalo to Albany there are four tracks (see page 52).   The West Shore* R.R., which it leases, runs nearly parallel with it to New York city.   Points where the two roads diverge will be mentioned as we go along.

The journey may start from Buffalo (1), the recent growth of

which has been marvellous even among American cities.

It is the largest coal-distributing point, and with Tonawanda, the largest lumber market in the world ; and is second in the world as a livestock market, a horse market,

---

* So called because it goes down the Hudson by the western shore, while the Central goes down by the eastern.

and a granary. It claims to be the cleanest, best-lighted, and healthiest city in the United States, with the best water and the best and most complete sewerage.

It is the gate to the northwest, not only by the steamers of the great lakes but also by the railways, four of the greatest of which, the Lake Shore and Michigan Southern, the New York, Chicago & St. Louis (Nickel Plate), the Michigan Central, and the Grand Trunk, have their terminal stations here. Already the third manufacturing city of the State, its possibilities under the power now secured from Niagara Falls (see page 23) can only be surmised. It is the seat of one of the State normal schools, of Canisius College, of several professional schools, and of a State Asylum for the Insane.

The 69 miles from Buffalo (1) to Rochester (5) is the least interesting stretch of country upon this railroad, but is broken midway by Batavia (2), a prosperous village, with large manufactures of farming machinery, and the seat of the State Institution for the Blind.

A branch of the New York Central from Tonawanda (37) to Canandaigua (46) crosses the main line at Batavia. The principal stations are Akron (43), LeRoy (44), and Honeoye Falls (45).

At Bergen (3) the West Shore R.R., which diverges from the Central at Buffalo (1) and passes through Akron (43), rejoins the Central, but at Chili Station (4) it diverges again, rejoining the Central at Fairport (6).

ROCHESTER (5) has been called both "The Flour City" and "The Flower City" from industries that have made it famous. The enormous water-power from the Genesee River (see page 24) makes it a natural manufacturing centre, and its location in the midst of some of the finest farming land in the State has made it a great distributing point.

The Erie Canal crosses the Genesee River here by an aqueduct 848 feet long.

Besides the University of Rochester and the Baptist Theological Seminary, the city has an Institution for Deaf Mutes, an Insane Asylum, and a State Industrial School of high repute. The Powers Building is a costly and handsome office-building, and contains a valuable art-gallery open to the public.

Formerly trains bound w. by the Michigan Central went from

Rochester to Niagara Falls (38) by the direct route, passing through Brockport (42), Albion (41), Medina (40), and Lockport (39); but now this road is used only for local traffic, all fast through trains being sent by way of Buffalo.

Brockport (42) is the seat of a State Normal School, and has manufactures of agricultural implements. Albion (41) is the county seat, and has flour mills, iron manufactures, and quarries. Medina (40) gives its name to a handsome mottled sandstone (see page 66) extensively used for building.

LOCKPORT (39) is named from the locks on the Erie Canal (see page 43), and gets abundant water power from the descent of the canal. There are also extensive quarries of Niagara limestone (see page 65). The railway crosses the canal by a viaduct 60 feet above the water.

The NIAGARA FALLS (38) have already been described (pp. 21–23). The city includes what was formerly the village of Suspension Bridge, and from the enormous water power now made available seems likely to become a great manufacturing centre.

There are branches of the Central from Lewiston, below Niagara Falls, to Buffalo, passing through Tonawanda (37), and from Lockport (39) to Tonawanda direct. The city of Buffalo (1) already reaches nearly to Tonawanda. If its territorial limits should be made as large as those of Chicago, it would swallow up Tonawanda and Niagara Falls as well.

The part of Tonawanda N. of the creek is a separate village, known as North Tonawanda. Tonawanda is an enormous lumber market and participates in the recent rapid growth of the eastern bank of the Niagara river.

There are two lines of the Central from Rochester (5) to Syracuse (11), known as the "Old" or Auburn Road, passing through Canandaigua (46), Geneva (48), and Auburn (52), and the "Direct Road", passing through Lyons (8). The fast through trains go by the latter.

A characteristic feature of the scenery on the Direct Road is the

alluvial hills, like that shown in the cut of the so-called Mormon Hill near Palmyra (7). To one accustomed to the rocky hills of New England, where tradition has it that the noses of sheep have to be sharpened to enable them to reach the grass between the stones, it is a surprise to see these hills plowed completely over, and to learn that their soil is more fertile than that of the plain below.

Fairport (6) has a variety of manufactures, including saleratus and baking-powder. Palmyra (7) is a handsome and wealthy village, with some manufactures and a considerable local trade.

Lyons (8) has distilleries of peppermint oil, a local product of considerable importance, with flour mills and other manufactures. A branch of the Central connects this village with Geneva (48).

Clyde (9) has a glass-factory and other manufactures. At Weedsport (10) is the crossing of the Southern Central railroad.

Returning now to Rochester and coming E. by the Auburn Road, the first large village is Canandaigua (46), with its wide main street and its adjoining lake among the most beautiful villages of the State. Clifton Springs (47) has a noted sanitarium already referred to (see page 57). Geneva (48) also has a spring and water-cure. This village is half-way between Rochester and Syracuse, and has an extensive steamboat traffic over Seneca Lake with Watkins. It is the seat of Hobart College. Waterloo (49) and Seneca Falls (50) have extensive manufactures. Cayuga (51) is the terminus of the Cayuga Lake branch of the Lehigh Valley railway.

AUBURN (52) is among the handsomest cities of the State. It has many manufactures, among them the most extensive in the country of reapers and mowing-machines. It is the seat of a theological seminary and of a State prison. It was the residence for many years of Wm. H. Seward.

Skaneateles Junction (53) is connected by a railway of 5 miles with Skaneateles, at the foot of the beautiful lake of that name (see page 36).

SYRACUSE (11) is often called "The Salt City", from what was once its greatest industry (see pages 56, 57), and "The Central City" from its location. As the junction of the Erie and the Oswego canals, and with four lines of railway to New York, it is a great distributing centre. Its manufactures are extensive, and they are diverse, so that its prosperity does not depend upon whether any one product happens to be up or down in the market.

It is the seat of Syracuse University, whose buildings, one of which, the Crouse College for Women is shown in the cut, may be seen from the train crowning the hill in the southeastern part of the city. Half-way up the southwestern hill may be seen the Institution for the Feeble-minded, which has a national reputation.

The view on the opposite page shows the crossing of the Erie Canal by Salina street, the principal street of the city, with an electric car-line extending from Onondaga Valley, four miles S., to Onondaga Lake, two miles N. The street which turns to cross the bridge is Genesee street, before the days of railroads the old turnpike between Buffalo and Albany. A little beyond this swing-bridge is the junction of the Erie with the Oswego Canal.

At Canastota (12) the West Shore diverges again from the Central, cutting straight across the country to Utica (15), without making the bend of the Central to the N. Oneida (13) has large manufactures, and is an extensive market for the hops that are in much of this region the principal product.

ROME (14) is the terminus of the Black River Canal, and has considerable manufactures.

It contains a State Institution for Deaf Mutes well-known for its excellent methods.

Half way from Rome to Utica may be seen on the right the monument erected near Oriskany a century after to commemorate the bloodiest battle of the Revolution, fought Aug. 6, 1777. For the proceedings at the celebration, Aug. 6, 1877, see "The Centennial Celebrations of the State of New York" (8:465, Albany, 1879), pp. 57-149, and Hendrick's "History of the Empire State", pp. 101, 102.

In an address delivered at Wells College in 1880, Gov. Seymour spoke as follows of the ride along this road :

To show in another light how intelligence will give us pleasure in the ordinary course of our lives, let us compare the day's experience of different persons travelling through our own State from its w. borders to the city of New York. Starting from the great cataract of Niagara, where even the most ignorant will feel the grandeur of the scene, the man with a reasonable knowledge of the State in which he lives, will see along the whole course of the journey objects which will constantly arrest his attention, recall facts in history or science, and which will engage his mind with healthful and instructive thoughts.

He will notice at the outset upon the s., the range of highlands, reaching from Lake Erie to the flanks of the Alleghany Mountains. Its elevation is not great, but in many ways it is the most remarkable water-shed upon the face of our globe.

When he crosses the Genesee River, he sees its currents hurrying to the n. to mingle with the cold water of the Gulf of St. Lawrence and the oceans which cover the Arctic regions, and he knows that its sources are interlocked with those of the Alleghany, which find their outlet in the tepid waters in the Gulf of Mexico, thus finding such distant destinations, although they start upon their courses from the same hill-tops.

A little farther on his course, he sees where, from the same range, the springs which feed the branches of the Susquehanna run down the s. slopes to the Chesapeake Bay, while from their n. declivities the affluents of the Mohawk traverse the valley which leads to the Hudson, and join with it in breaking through the Alleghany ranges, which are not elsewhere severed from their uplifts in Georgia to their termination in Nova Scotia, a distance of more than a thousand miles.

These rivers and mountains recall to his memory their controlling influences over savage and civilized history. The Indian tribes who dwelt upon these hills made them strongholds for defence ; while the valleys, cut into deep channels by the rivers I have named, gave them pathways into the territories of their enemies. Their positions made them conquerors and masters of a large share of the regions E. of the Mississippi. The mind of the intelligent traveller will be led to reflections upon the influence of this Indian power upon the history and civilization of our country. But for this topography, and its influence upon Indian polity and power, the civilization of the whole valley of the Mississippi might have been of French and not of English aspects.

His mind will dwell upon all the events of the struggle running through a century, between France and Britain, for the control of this Continent ; their efforts, by diplomacy or force, to gain the support of the Iroquois ; the succession of military campaigns in this then remote wilderness by disciplined armies ; and the final overthrow of French power.

The highlands of Onondaga will recall the story of the French missionaries, who, in their religious zeal, penetrated the interior of our State, before the Colony of Virginia was formed, and will also remind him of the march of Champlain with his forces into its central regions, before the Dutch settled upon the Hudson, or the Pilgrims landed on Plymouth Rock. The earliest traces of European civilization in the original States of our Union, are to be found on the hills s. of Syracuse. Arms and implements used by Spanish and French explorers, and traces of fortifications, relics of religions and of funeral rites, show that civilized men attempted occupation of our territory many years before efforts were made by the English to plant colonies on the Atlantic coast.

In the county of Oneida, the site of Fort Stanwix and a view of the battle field of Oriskany, lead his mind on to the Revolutionary struggle, which followed the same pathways, marked by savage warfare, or by the contests of European ambition.

Along the valley of the Mohawk, the presence of the German population, seated there 150 years ago by the British government, will tell him of the great struggle against Louis the Great for dominion in Europe, which was finally defeated by the victories of Marlborough. The old churches built before the Revolution, for the use of the Palatines, and which were made places of refuge for the people against the barbarous warfare of Brant and his savage hordes, will remind him of the terrible history of a valley which suffered from the ravages of war, from the torch, the tomahawk and the scalping knife.

The old stone mansion of Sir William Johnson will recall the story of Indian treaties and his wonderful influence over the savage tribes.

The city of Albany, near the confluence of the Mohawk and the Hudson ; its important strategetic position through nearly two centuries ; the highlands of the Hudson, the strong defences of American liberty ; the treason of Arnold ; the wonderful passage through the chains of the Alleghany range, which leads the ocean tides w. of barriers which elsewhere cut off the Atlantic coast from the great interior of our continent, will give material for thought and reflection.

These and much more that I could mention, will occupy the mind of the intelligent traveller with subjects of natural and political interest ; they will engage his attention with topics of dignity and value. When he reaches the end of his journey, at the harbor of New York, he will feel that he has gained and not lost a day.

Utica (15) is one of the handsomest cities of the State, and a large manufacturing centre. It is also the centre of trade of the cheese-factories and other diary interests of central New York.

Its State Lunatic Asylum is one of the most noted in the world, and a Masonic Home has recently been established here.

From this point on to Rotterdam Junction (21) the West Shore follows the s. bank of the Mohawk, while the Central follows the N. bank.

Herkimer (16), at the junction of West Canada Creek, is a prosperous manufacturing village. It is connected by horse-cars with Mohawk, Ilion and Frankfort, on the other side of the Mohawk. The four villages are almost continuous. Ilion is noted for the Remington guns and typewriters made there.

The location of Little Falls (17) has already been described (pp. 15, 19, 27, 53). The water falls 44 feet in ¾ of a mile, affording abundant power for varied manufactures. It is also a centre of the dairy trade.

A local railway makes a double curve northeast to Dolgeville, a manufacturing village of phenomenal growth, largely inhabited by Germans. Its chief products are piano supplies and felt goods.

Palatine Bridge (18) takes its name from the old wooden bridge over the Mohawk connecting it with Canajoharie.

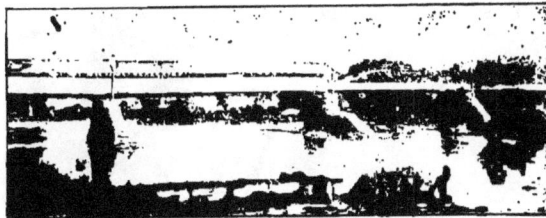

Fonda (19) is the southern terminus of the railway to Northville through Johnstown and Gloversville, the last named from the glove industry to which these towns are largely devoted. The village on the s. of the river is Fultonville.

AMSTERDAM (20) is largely given to the manufacture of knit-goods, carpets, boilers, and furniture. Its recent growth has been rapid.

At Rotterdam Junction (21) the West Shore turns s., cutting across to Coeyman's (24) on the Hudson. Here it connects with the Fitchburg R.R. running across to Mechanics ville (55), going on to Boston by way of Schaghticoke, Eagle Bridge, and Hoosick Falls, and about half-way to Coeyman's, at Voorheesville (25), it connects with the Delaware and Hudson, running its cars over that road to Albany and Saratoga Springs. Below Coeyman's it follows the western bank of the Hudson to Weehawken, N. J., where ferries connect it with 42d street and Franklin street, New York city.

SCHENECTADY (22) has manufactures of locomotives and brooms, and has recently grown rapidly through the large electrical works established there.

It is the seat of Union University. The Central here crosses the Mohawk and bears off to the southeast for Albany, by the heaviest grade on the line ; but a branch follows the s. bank of the river to Cohoes, and crosses the Hudson at Green Island to Troy (54). Schenectady is the usual connection from the w. for Saratoga.

ALBANY (23) is the capital of the State. As the junction of the Erie and the Champlain canals with the Hudson, and of the Central with the Delaware & Hudson Canal Co., and Boston and the Albany railways, with two bridges across the Hudson, it is an important shipping-point, especially for grain and lumber. It also has large manufactures, and its eternally unfinished State capitol gives employment to a multitude of laborers.

More than 20 millions has been expended upon this structure, shown on the hill in the opposite cut, and the present estimate of the cost of completion is 5 millions more.

The State Normal College is here, as are also the Dudley Observatory, and the medical, pharmaceutical, and law departments of Union University (see page 74).

Besides the railways on both sides of the river, Albany is connected with New York by two lines of fine steamers, one running in the day time and the other at night, and both favorite routes in summer. The picture on the following page of the Hudson river at Albany shows at the left the Dean Richmond lying at dock.

HUDSON (26) is on a steep bluff above the river, 60 feet high, and the principal street is along a ridge to Prospect Hill, 450 feet higher. It has blast furnaces, and manufactures of clothing, paper, steam fire-engines, etc.

A steam ferry across the river connects it with Athens, to which a branch road runs down from Coxsackie. Helderberg limestone is quarried here and burned for lime.

All the way down from Albany the Catskill mountains have been in sight and Catskill (27) is the station for this famous summer resort. It was along the road from Catskill to the Mountain House that Rip Van Winkle took his long nap, and saw the impish ninepins. A railway runs to Cairo, and to the Catskill Mountain House.

Rhinecliff is the station on the Central from which one crosses the river to KINGSTON (28), which includes within its city limits what was formerly the village of Rondout. It has large quarries of flagstone, and is the centre of a large cement industry.

It was here that the temporary State congress adopted the Constitution of the State.

POUGHKEEPSIE (29) is upon a plain 200 feet above the river.   It is half-way between Albany and New York and the second largest city between them.

The new bridge shown in the following cut of the Philadelphia, Reading and New

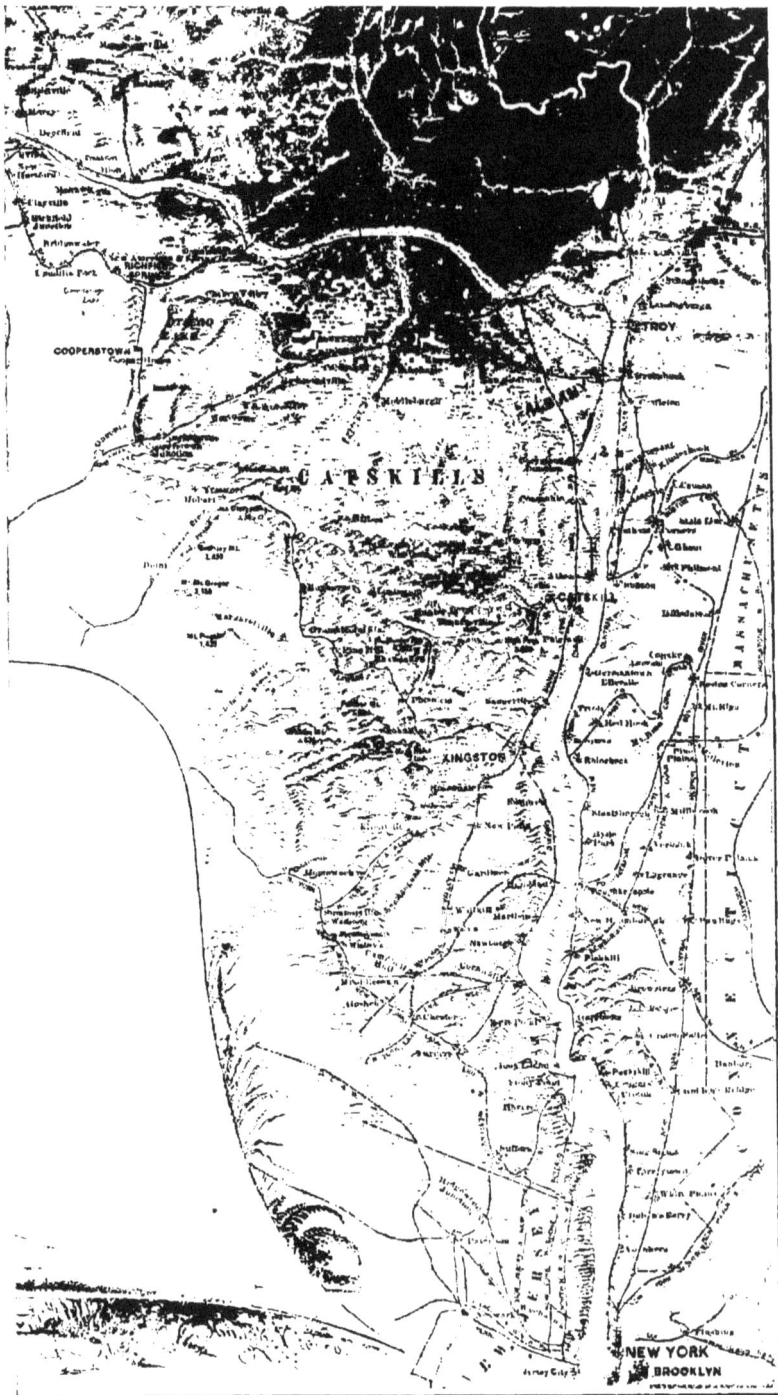

England railway is 6,767¼ feet or more than 1¼ miles long, being second in size only to that over the Firth of Forth in Scotland.

This railway starts from Campbell Hall, runs through the rich farms of Orange and Ulster counties nearly parallel with the Wallkill Valley road, shown on the opposite map, to Highland, opposite Poughkeepsie, and then turns E., crossing the river. It then runs parallel with the Poughkeepsie & Eastern, formerly the Poughkeepsie, Hartford & Boston, to Pine Plains, and then N. to its Rhinecliff branch, formerly the Hartford & Connecticut Western, by which it curves around Copake to the s., crosses the Harlem at Boston Corners, where the three States meet, the terminus of the P. & E., and goes on to Hartford, by way of Canaan and Winsted, through some of the most charming scenery in Connecticut.

A branch of this road runs south-east from Poughkeepsie to Hopewell Junction, on the Newburgh, Dutchess & Connecticut road, at the junction of the New York & New England. The N. D. & C. runs from Fishkill, through Matteawan, to Pine Plains, where it turns E. and meets the P. R. & N. E. at Millerton. The N. Y. & N. E. runs parallel with the N. D. & C. to Hopewell, and then bears to the southeast through Brewsters, running to Hartford through Danbury and Waterbury.

Fishkill is the scene of many of the exploits of Harvey Birch, in Cooper's "Spy".

Poughkeepsie is the seat of Vassar College, a noted college for women, shown in the cut, and of the Hudson River State Hospital for the Insane.

From Highland an electric railway runs to New Paltz, where one of the State normal schools is located. This is the route from Poughkeepsie to Lakes Mohonk and Minnewaska.

NEWBURGH (30) is reached from the Central by steam ferry from Fishkill-on-the-Hudson. Its site rises steeply some 300 feet from the river (see page 28), and is bounded on the s. by the deep ravine of a small creek that flows into the Hudson. The residences on the southeast bluff have a view that can hardly be surpassed. The scenery on river from here to Peekskill is much the finest on the river.

Newburgh is the northern terminus of the Erie railway and has considerable shipping-trade upon the river.

Washington's Headquarters are preserved as a State park. The original house is shown in the circle on the left, while the arch is erected as a memorial. The grounds are visited by thousands every year, as it is a favorite excursion-point. The house is filled with revolutionary relics.

A little further down the river reached from the Central by ferry from Garrison, is West Point (31), the nation's military school, views

of which are here given.   Its situation is perhaps the finest in America. A view looking N. is shown on page 28.

As the river emerges from the Highlands, we reach Peekskill (32), a growing village with considerable manufacturing. Soon the river broadens into Tappan Bay, often named Haverstraw Bay from Haverstraw (33) on the western bank, with considerable brick manufacturing industries Further down on that side is Nyack (35) with varied manufactures. Across the river are Sing Sing (34) with its State prison, and further down Tarrytown, whence the steam ferry runs to Nyack.

Now we reach the Palisades (see page 27), that extend on the W. side of the river the rest of the way to New York. The eastern bank is mostly covered by costly suburban residences and the villages of Irvington (36) and Dobbs Ferry are but continuations of the cities below of which they will soon be a part. Near Irvington is Sunnyside, shown in the cut, the home of Washington Irving.

YONKERS (37) is already connected with New York by elevated train, and is practically continuous with it. Its carpet, silk, and hat manufactures are extensive, and it makes also mowing-machines and elevators.

The drive to New York is delightful, for the road is a handsome boulevard, and Morningside Park, shown in the cut, with the river and the Palisades on the one hand and beautiful residences on the other can hardly be surpassed. It may pass by the new grounds of Columbia College, with which the Teachers' College and Barnard College are connected, with new buildings on a scale of cost and with a harmony of architecture not hitherto attempted in America. It may then turn off to the southeast and extend through Central Park with its Museum of Natural History and its Metropolitan Art Museum. Emerging at 59th street, the ride may continue down Fifth Avenue, the fashionable residence street of the city.

Going by the railway, the train soon turns from the Hudson, follows Spuyten Duyvil Creek, recently converted into a ship-canal, and turning again to cross the Harlem follows down Manhattan Island, with glimpses on the right of Central Park, to the well-known 42d street station, also the terminus of the Harlem and of the New Haven railways. It is the only terminal railway station on Manhattan Island. From this station without going outside the roof one may take the elevated railway to the Battery, and by its connections to almost all parts of New York.

NEW YORK (38) is the largest city on the western continent, and after it has been extended like London and Paris to cover the territory legitimately associated with it, is not unlikely within the life of readers of this book to be in population the greatest of all cities.

NEW YORK BAY.

As a business centre, New York is second only to London. The cut shows Wall street, the bankers' headquarters, with Trinity church at its head, and the United States sub-treasury on the right. The statue in front is that of Washington, on the site of Federal Hall, where in 1789 he delivered his first inaugural address.

A bird's-eye view on page 61 shows the general outlines of the city. In the right-hand lower corner is Brooklyn, connected with New York by the East River bridge. In the left hand lower corner is Governor's Island. The park seen in the left-hand lower corner of the city is the Battery ; the round building formerly called Castle Garden, the landing-place of immigrants till this was transferred to Ellis Island (see page 60), is now used as an aquarium. From this point the street extending through the two tallest rows of buildings, parallel with the river, is Broadway. The church on the left is Trinity, already pictured at the head of Wall street. The large building with a dome is the Post Office, near which are the great newspaper buildings of the *World*, and *Tribune*, and *Times*. The large building with a square tower between the Post Office and the East River is the Corn Exchange.

The view on the opposite page is from a different point. It shows Battery Park, and Broadway following up the Island nearly parallel with the Hudson.

2. By the New York, Lake Erie and Western (Erie)

The map on page 20 shows the five great river divisions of the State. The Erie railway, reaching from New York to Dunkirk, its original terminus, had to cut its way through all five of these divisions, and yet followed the banks of streams almost all the way,—an engineering feat which in 1851 was marvellous. See map on page 96.

Starting from Jersey City (1), the road strikes off to the N. through New Jersey, crossing into New York just before it reaches Suffern (2), the junction of the Piermont (36) branch, which has an extension to Nyack. At Newburgh Junction (3) the main road turns w., while a branch continues N. to Newburgh (37), already mentioned (see page 90). From Grey court (4) is another connecting line to Newburgh. Goshen (5) is an important dairy centre. From here branches run s. through Florida to Pine Island (38) and N. to Montgomery (39), and the P. P. & B. railway runs through to Campbell Hall.

MIDDLETOWN (6) has manufactures of wool hats, blankets, carpet-bags, and saws. The State Homeopathic Insane Hospital is here.

The New York, Ontario and Western crosses the Erie here, and the New Jersey Midland terminates here. A branch of the Erie runs N. 13 miles to Pine Bush (40).

The railway now crosses the Shawangunk mountains, passing out of the Hudson River into the Delaware system, and at Port Jervis (7) reaches the junction of two rivers and of three States (see page 30).

A railway 24 miles long connects Port Jervis with Monticello (41), 1387 feet above

sea level and a favorite summer resort. A view along this road near the hotel at Huguenot, is given on the opposite page. A branch of this road runs

from Huguenot Junction to Wurtsboro and Summitville, connecting with the New York, Ontario and Western.

The view here given shows the Delaware as seen from Hawks Nest Rocks, 6 miles w. of Port Jervis. The Rocks are shown in the lower portion of the cut. The canal on the right is that of the Delaware & Hudson Canal Co., running from Honesdale, Pa., to Rondout.

The railway now crosses the Delaware into Pennsylvania, following the s. bank of the river for 30 miles to Tuston, with a branch at Lackawaxen (8) for the coal mines at Honesdale.

It then crosses to the northern bank of the Delaware and follows it through Narrowsburg (9). thus named because the river is here compressed by two points of rock into a channel so narrow that the water is 100 feet deep, and Hancock (10), to Deposit (11), where it parts from the Delaware, crossing the watershed over into the Susquehanna system. To do this it strikes down into Pennsylvania again.

Susquehanna (12) is the junction of its branch running down to the coal mines of Carbondale.

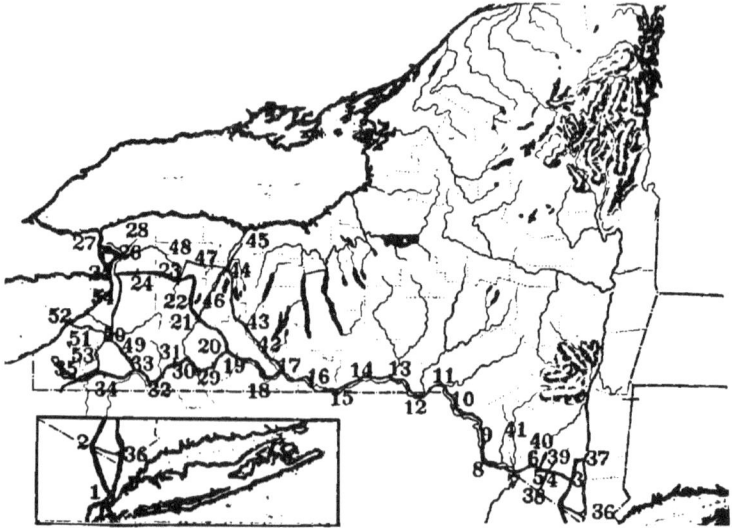

It now follows the Susquehanna as faithfully as it did the Delaware. It crosses the Chenango at BINGHAMTON (13), called "The Parlor City" from its cleanliness, and growing rapidly.

There is here a State Hospital for the Insane, and an Institution for Inebriates.

It passes through Owego (14), and at Waverly (15) almost touches the Pennsylvania boundary.

Here it says adieu to the Susquehanna, and follows its tributary, the Chemung, to ELMIRA (16), an attractive city, with large manufactures, especially of iron.

Here are Elmira College, the first college for women ever established; and the Elmira Reformatory, whose system of reclaiming criminals is widely known.

A branch from Elmira runs w. of s. to the coal region of Blossburg and Hoytville, Pa.

The railway strikes N. and makes a right angle at Horseheads, coming back to the river and following it on the s. side to CORNING (17).

This is the terminus of several branches of the Fall Brook coal system of railways, connecting the mines of Lycoming and Tioga counties with the New York Central railway system. It has large manufactures, and its artistic cut-glass is highly esteemed.

At Painted Post, two miles further, where the Cohocton and Tioga rivers unite (see page 32), the Rochester (45) division of the Erie branches off from the main line. The principal stations are Bath (42), the seat of the State Soldiers' Home; Avoca, Cohocton, Blood's (post-office Atlanta) (43), Wayland, Conesus, near the lake of that name, and Avon (44). The last has been spoken of (page 57).

Local railways run from Bath (42) northeast to Hammondsport, at the head of Keuka Lake (see page 34); and from Kanona N. to Prattsburgh.

A branch runs s. from Avon to Mount Morris (46), with connections for Dansville. Two beautiful views of the Genesee valley near Dansville are shown on page 108.

Another branch runs E. through LeRoy (47) to Batavia (48), for which see page 78 ; and hence through Alexander to the main line at Attica (23).

Taking the southern of the two branches of the Chemung, the railway follows the Tioga, passing through Andover (18) and Canisteo (19) to Hornellsville (20), pre-eminently a railroad city, but with some manufactures.

Here the original road ran on to Dunkirk (52), which in 1851 was expected to be the great port on Lake Erie. But its docks are rotting now, and the fast trains of the Erie run to Buffalo (25), or by direct connection w. by way of Jamestown (35).

The Buffalo division surmounts the watershed just before reaching Nunda Station, almost at the boundary between Allegany and Livingston counties, and celebrates its reaching the St. Lawrence system by crossing Portage Falls (21) on a picturesque iron bridge 820 feet long and 236 feet above the river. See page 23.

At Silver Springs (22) is the junction for Silver Lake, 3 miles long and becoming recognized as a charming summer resort ; and for Perry at its outlet.

Attica (23) is a railroad centre, with a tannery, carriage-shops, and flour-mill. At Lancaster (24) the Erie comes into Buffalo (25) parallel with the Central through a suburban region rapidly building up.

The road is continued to Tonawanda (26) and Niagara Falls (27), with a branch to Lockport (28)—all of these parallel with the similar lines on the Central (see page 79).

Returning to Hornellsville (20) and following the Erie w. we curve to the s., and cross the watershed into the St. Lawrence system, reaching Dyke Creek at Andover (29), and following it to its junction with the Genesee at Wellsville (30), the largest village in Allegany county and an important shipping-point.

The railway follows down the Genesee, crossing it at Belmont (which includes tooth-picks among its manufactures), but at Belvidere, at the mouth of Van Campen's Creek, makes a sharp turn to the s. and follows up that stream beyond Friendship, crosses the watershed into the Ohio system, and at Cuba (31) strikes Oil Spring Creek, which it follows down to its junction with Ischua Creek near Hinsdale, and thence follows the Ischua, now called Olean Creek, to its junction with the Allegany River at Olean (32), which was made a city in 1894.

The railway now follows the Allegany to Salamanca (33), which is in the Indian Reservation (see page 69).

From here the original main line extended to Dunkirk (64), following up the deep valley of Little Valley Creek beyond Little Valley (49), crossing the watershed into the St. Lawrence system, and following a branch of the Cattaraugus, crossing the Buffalo and Southwestern division of the Erie at Dayton (50), and passing through Forestville (51).

Dunkirk (52) has an excellent harbor, and was once thought to have a great future. But its commerce has gone to Buffalo, and its largest industry is the Brooks Locomotive Works, employing more than 1000 men.

It is the northern terminus of the Dunkirk, Allegheny Valley & Pittsburg railway, which passes through Fredonia, three miles away, where there is a State Normal School, and which was lighted by natural gas so far back as in 1821 (see page 59). It is also connected with Fredonia by an electric railway.

A branch runs from Salamanca s. through Bradford, Pa., to Johnsonburgh, Pa.

At Red House the Erie turns off w., following the valley of Little Connewango Creek, through Randolph (44) to Kennedy, where it strikes across to JAMESTOWN (35) near the foot of Chautauqua Lake, the outlet of which furnishes water-power for extensive and diverse manufactures. Thence the Erie extends southwest into Pennsylvania to Corry, Meadville, Warren, etc., and makes western connections.

The Buffalo and Southwestern division of the Erie runs parallel with the main line from Jamestown (35) beyond Kennedy into Cattaraugus county, and then turns N., passing through Conewango, Cherry Creek (53), Dayton (50) and Hamburg (54).

3. THE ROME, WATERTOWN & OGDENSBURG

This line was in 1891 leased in perpetuity to the New York Central, but is extensive and distinctive enough to require separate map and treatment. It is the St. Lawrence river route from the w. to northern New England, and besides controlling much of the local traffic of New York, its through trains are well patronized.

Starting from Niagara Falls (1), where it connects with the Michigan Central, and following the river down to Lewiston (2), the head of navigation, it turns off to the E., running nearly parallel with the lake shore to Watertown.

Along the s. shore the villages are mostly small, Wilson (3), Lyndonville (4), and Kendall (5) being the largest till Charlotte (6) is reached, the lake port of Rochester, with a population of 1500, and the centre of several attractive summer resorts, including Ontario Beach, Windsor Beach, Lake Bluff, Sea Breeze, Irondequoit Bay, Lake Beach and Lake View. A branch line connects the R. W. & O. with Rochester, 7 miles s.

At Charlotte (6) the railway crosses the Genesee by an iron-drawbridge 300 feet long.

Passing Ontario (7) and Sodus, the line crosses at Wallingford (8), the Sodus branch of the Pennsylvania railway. Wolcott (10) has a thousand inhabitants, and Red Creek, 6 miles further E., has half as many.

At Sterling (10) is the crossing of the Southern Central branch of the Lehigh Valley.

OSWEGO (11) is, next to Toronto, the largest city on Lake Ontario. It has a good harbor, formed by the mouth of the Oswego River, and is protected by Fort Ontario. The site is bounded on the s. by a bluff 160 feet high.

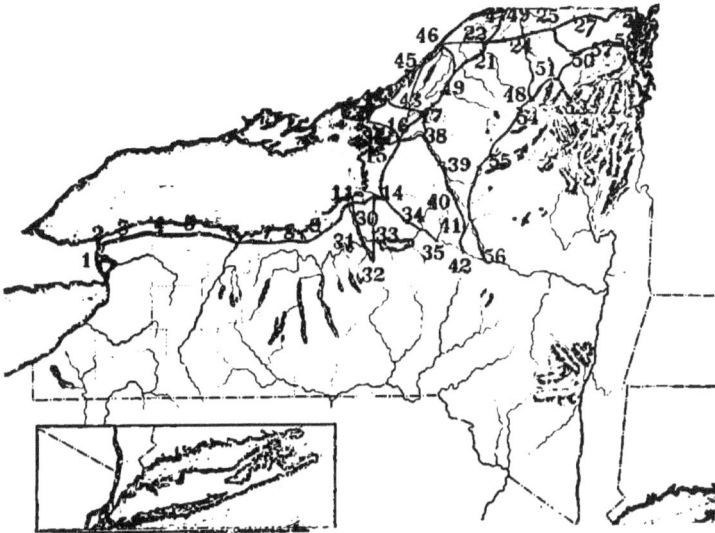

For its water-power see page 25 ; for its mineral spring, page 57. Its State Normal School is one of the most famous in the world. Among its manufactures that of corn-starch is best known, its once famous flour-mills having been mostly burned. As the terminus of the Oswego Canal and with its fine harbor it might be expected to have considerable commerce, but its principal shipments are of coal.

A branch line runs down the eastern bank of the river to Syracuse (32). The principal stations are Fulton (30), the water-power of which is mentioned on page 25 ; and Phœnix (31), on the Oswego Canal, with some manufactures.

Mexico (12) has a tannery and flouring mills, and an academy at one time quite prominent in the State. At Pulaski the road reaches the Salmon River, and follows it for a little distance on its way to Richland (14). This river must be carefully distinguished from the other river of the same name, which this railway crosses at Malone. See next page.

From Pulaski a branch runs s. to Syracuse (32), with no large stations. At Central Square (33) is the crossing of the New York, Ontario and Western. At the crossing of the Oneida River at Brewerton there is a view from the train of Oneida Lake.

At Richland (14) is the junction with the Rome (35) division, the principal station on which is Camden (34). This is the starting-point of the Elmira, Cortland & Northern railway. See page 116.

Adams (15) has a foundry and machine shop, and is a distributing-point for farm supplies.

WATERTOWN (16) gets its water-power from the falls of the Black River (see page 49), and has extensive manufactures of flour, leather, machinery, woolen goods, sewing machines, and spring wagons.

It is pleasantly situated and attractively built up.

Branches run from here to Sackett's Harbor (36), Cape Vincent (37), and Carthage (38), the last connecting with the Utica and Black River division, which the main line crosses again at Philadelphia (17).

This was formerly a rival railway, from Utica (42) to Ogdensburg (46). Starting at Utica (42) it bends around to Trenton Falls (41), crosses the Black River Canal at Boon-

ville (40), and follows the river through Low-
ville (39) to Carthage (38). Continuing N. it
crosses the main line at Philadelphia (17)
and at Theresa Junction (43) connects for
Clayton (44) and the Thousand Islands (see
page 63) and goes on through Morristown
(45) to Ogdensburg (46).

Antwerp (18) contains what was once the
Black River Conference Seminary, now Ives
Seminary. Gouverneur (19) has important manufactures and quarries. At De Kalb
Junction (20) a branch runs through Rensselaer Falls and Heuvelton to Ogdensburg
(46). The St. Lawrence is here 2 miles wide, and in winter may usually be crossed on
the ice to Prescott, on the Canadian shore. It has large manufactures of flour, lumber,
machinery, and leather, and a State Hospital for the Insane.

After passing Canton, the county seat, where the St. Lawrence University is located,
the train reaches Potsdam (21), which gives its name to the hard red sandstone quarried
here. It has extensive lumber-mills, and a State Normal School.

Norwood (22) is the Junction of the R. W. & O. with the Central
Vermont, by which it makes its eastern connections.

The R. W. & O. continues to Massena Springs (47), spoken of on page 57. The
length of the line from Niagara Falls is 301 miles.

Considering the Central Vermont as a continuation of the R. W. & O., we turn now
to this road. It starts from Ogdensburg (46), and passing through Madrid, N. of which
are Madrid Springs, takes the through cars of the R. W. & O. at Norwood (22), crosses
the St. Regis River at Winthrop (23), spoken of on page 49, and the Northern Adirondack road at Moira (24).

This road is used mostly for transporting lumber, though it has stations for Paul
Smith's and for Saranac Inn. It ends at Tupper Lake (48). A branch of the Central
Vermont runs N. to Bombay (49), where it connects with a branch of the Grand Trunk
from Massena Springs (47) into Canada.

The Central Vermont reaches the Salmon River at Malone (25), the
largest village on its New York line, and one of the pleasantest towns
in the State. It has an Institution for Deaf Mutes.

Here connection is made with the Adirondack & St. Lawrence railway, also leased
by the N. Y. Central. Following up the Salmon River to Loon Lake (50), this road follows the watershed between the St. Lawrence and Hudson systems (see page 37), connecting at Saranac Junction (51) for Saranac Lake (52) and Lake Placid (53). It then
curves around by Rowlin's Pond, crossing the Northern Adirondack at Tupper Lake
Junction (48), crosses the Racket River before reaching Childwold (54), strikes down
through a corner of Hamilton county, nearing the Fulton chain of lakes at Fulton
Chain (55), strikes S. to Trenton Falls (41), and then bears off to the southeast till it
meets the New York Central at Herkimer (56). See relief map on page 102.

The Chateaugay railway extends from Saranac Lake (52), through Loon Lake (50),
curves off to the E., passes through Dannemora (57), where there is a State Prison, and
ends at Plattsburgh (58).

The Central Vermont continues through Chateaugay (26), the
nitrogen springs of which were spoken of on page 57, and Ellenburgh
(27), crosses the New York and Canada at Mooer's (28), and reaches the
boundary of the State at Rouse's Point (29), on the Canadian frontier.

It crosses Lake Champlain on a bridge a mile long, and continues through St. Albans,
Montpelier, and White River Junction, Vt., to points E.

4. The Delaware and Hudson R. R.

We have now followed the three* great lines that cross the State horizontally, and we come to those which cross the State perpendicularly. These are in some respects even more interesting than the others, as they cut through the geological strata of the State, and show a constant change of soil and of scenery.

The longest of these is the Delaware and Hudson R.R., which

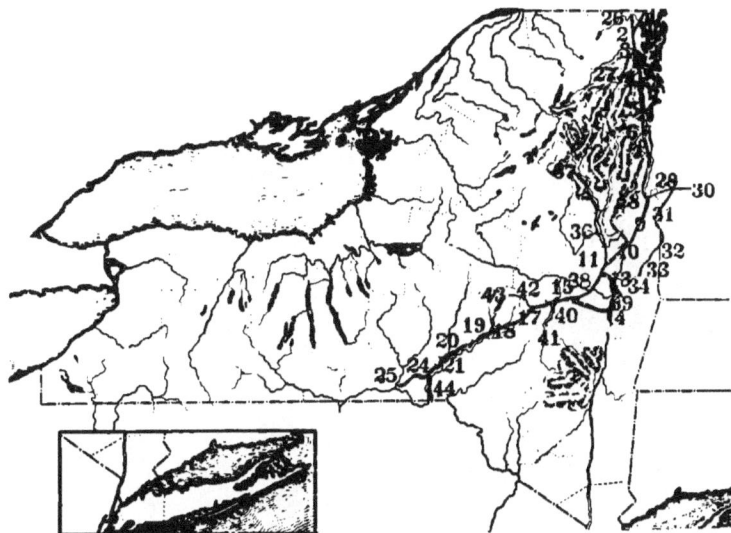

reaches from Rouse's Point to Binghamton, 333 miles.

This road takes its name from the Delaware & Hudson Canal Co., which built the canal from Honesdale to Rondout (see page 75), and afterward got control of what used to be the Albany & Susquehanna and the Rensselaer & Saratoga railways, with their connections.

Starting from the Canada line at Rouse's Point (1) and connecting at Chazy Junction (2) with its line for Mooer's Junction (26), it reaches Plattsburgh (3) on Cumberland Bay, where Commodore McDonough won his great victory over the British in 1814. See Hendrick's History, pp. 134, 135.

This village has a safe harbor, and abundant water-power from the Saranac. It has a State Normal School.

A branch road runs to Au Sable Forks† (27), affording a pleasant route to Au Sable Chasm on the E., and to Whiteface Mountain and Lake Placid on the W.

It follows the shore of Lake Champlain to Port Kent (4) where there is a branch road for Au Sable Chasm (see page 50), and soon

*Four, if the West Shore be considered apart from the New York Central.
†The train stops at Rogers Station, (Clintonville post-office), 3 miles from the village.

runs farther inland to Westport (5), whence there is a delightful stage-ride mountainward to Elizabethtown.

At Port Henry (6) it reaches the great iron region, with a branch freight road running up to Moriah and Mineville. At Crown Point, 8 miles further, there is a branch road, also for iron, to Hammondville.

At Addison Junction (7) it forms connection for Ticonderoga (28) and Lake George, and with the Central Vermont for Leicester Junction and other Vermont points.

Here steamer passengers are now transferred. Before the railway was built the steamers used to run up the narrow head of the lake to Whitehall (8).

This village is picturesquely located at the foot of Skene's Mountain and at the mouth of Wood Creek, and is the terminus of the Champlain Canal. It was once a leading lumber market and still does considerable lumber trade. Its principal manufacture is of silk.

A branch line runs E. from Whitehall to Rutland, Vt. (30), connecting at Castleton (29) with a branch of the D. & H. that runs through Granville (31), Salem (32), and Cambridge (33), and connects with the Fitchburg R.R. at Eagle Bridge (34). The hilly character of the centre of Washington County is shown from the fact that so long a railway journey is necessary to go from the eastern to the western part. A branch road runs up from Johnsonville to Greenwich.

The railway now crosses the watershed to the Hudson system by following the Champlain Canal through Fort Ann (9) to Fort Edward (10), where connection is made for Glens Falls and Lake George. See page 44.

It crosses the Hudson and strikes inland to Saratoga Springs (11), already spoken of on page 57.

Here connection is made with the Adirondack branch of the D. & H., which runs through Corinth (35), with its huge paper-mills; Luzerne (36), or Hadley, as it used to be called, at the junction of the Sacondaga, with the highest falls on the Hudson; and so on up the river till at North Creek (37), 57 miles from Saratoga, it lands its passengers well within the portals of the Adirondacks. See map on the opposite page.

A branch of the Fitchburg R.R., runs from Saratoga Springs by Saratoga Lake to Mechanicsville, with a branch to Victory Mills and Schuylerville, on the Hudson. Near Schuylerville is the Saratoga Monument, here shown, erected Oct. 17, 1877, to commemorate Burgoyne's surrender a century before, the most important event of the Revolutionary War. See "Centennial Celebrations", pp. 231-356.

At Bemus Heights, at the head of Saratoga Lake, the centenary of the battle fought there was celebrated Sept. 19, 1877. See "Centennial Celebrations", pp. 151-194, and Hendrick's History, p. 103.

A road runs from Saratoga Springs up Mt. McGregor, where Gen. Grant died.

At Ballston (12), already spoken of on page 57, the railway forks, one branch connecting with the Central for the w. at Schenectady (38), and with the main line of the D. & H. at Quaker Street (15); while the other, on which the through trains are run,

curving southeast to Mechanicsville, whence it follows the Hudson through Waterford, Cohoes, and West Troy to Albany (14). See pages 85, 88.

Cars for New York and the E. are switched at Green Island, a village on the island of that name in the Hudson opposite Troy, for TROY (39), at the Mouth of Poestenkill Creek, and at the head of navigation on the Hudson.

The site of the city is an alluvial plain extending 3 miles along the river, and from ½ to ¾ miles wide. The city is fast creeping up the hills on the E. however, and Mount Ida, on the southeast, from which the view on the opposite page is taken, has a delightful outlook in every direction. The city has extensive manufactures, especially of iron, and of collars and cuffs.

It was here that Emma Willard established her Female Seminary, the first institution founded for the higher education of women, which has recently received large endowments for new buildings. Here too is the Rensselaer Polytechnic Institute, shown in the cut, one of the best scientific schools in the country.

St. Joseph's Theological Provincial Seminary has a sightly location upon the hill. Across the river, at West Troy, is a large national arsenal. A line of night steamers to New York is well patronized in summer.

From Albany (14), where the station adjoins that of the New York

Central, but is between it and the river, and lower, the railway curves off to the w., crossing the West Shore at Voorheesville, and connecting with its Schenectady branch at Quaker Street (15).

When it reaches Schoharie Creek at Central Bridge, it connects with a branch road following the creek up through Schoharie (40) to Middleburgh (41).

At Schoharie (40) is the Old Fort, still in state of preservation but with the marks of cannon-balls, which in Oct., 1780 preserved its inmates from an attack by a strong force of Indians, Tories, and soldiers. Here on Sept. 23, 1876, was laid the corner-stone of a monument to David Williams, one of the captors of André, the British spy. See "Centennial Celebrations", pp. 195-230, and Hendrick's History, pp. 107, 108.

From Central Bridge the railway follows the Cobleskill Creek to West Richmondville, surmounts the watershed into the Susquehanna system almost at the county line, and follows Schenevus Creek through Worcester and Schenevus (18) to its junction with the Susquehanna, where a line runs N. through Hartwick Seminary to Cooperstown (43), already mentioned on page 42.

Passing by Howe's Cave (16), described on pages 54, 55, it connects at Cobleskill (17) for Sharon Springs (42), mentioned on page 57, and Cherry Valley (43).

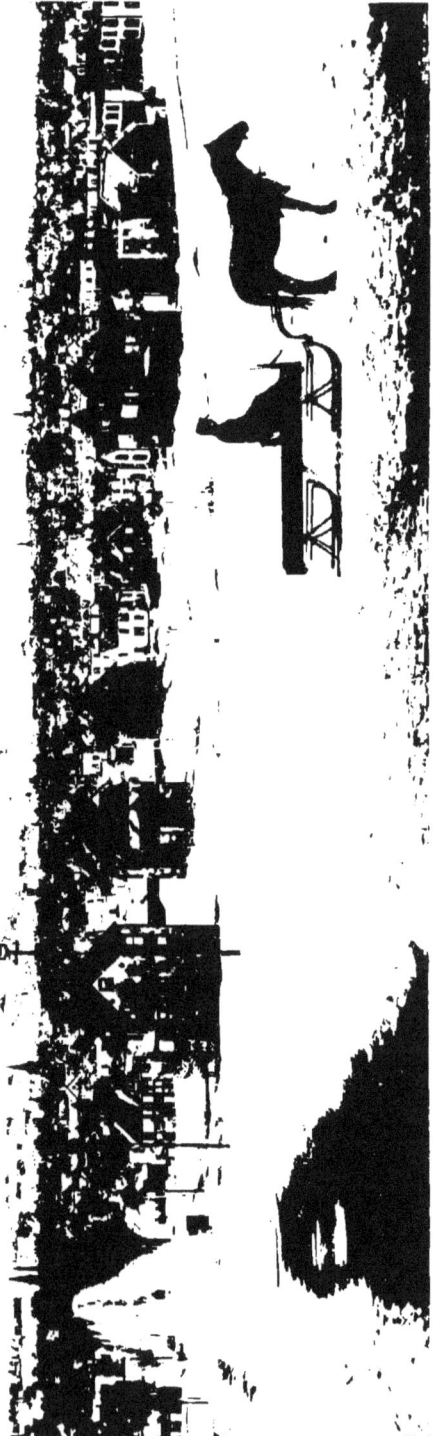

Here the Cherry Valley Monument was unveiled Aug. 15, 1877, to commemorate the massacre of Nov., 1778. See "Centennial Celebrations", pp. 357-383, and Hendrick's History, p. 105.

Following now the Susquehanna, it passes through Oneonta (19), the largest village between Albany and Binghamton, and a natural distributing-point for a rich farming section.

It is the seat of a State Normal School, the view from the steps of which given on the opposite page shows the Susquehanna valley at its best. This outlook is said to resemble strikingly the valley of Lacedaemon, in Greece.

The seclusion of this valley between its hills is shown from the fact that the quickest way to reach Oneonta from New York city or from Syracuse is by way of either Albany or Binghamton. Compare what is said of crossing mountains on page 112.

Passing through Unadilla (20), and barely cutting across the corner of Delaware county, the railway crosses at Sidney (21) the New York, Ontario and Western ; passes through Bainbridge (22) and Afton (23) ; and at Nineveh (24) diverges from the river, strikes northwest, cuts through the hill by a tunnel, and curves down into Binghamton (25). See page 96.

A branch from Nineveh (24) follows the Susquehanna through Windsor (44) down, into Pennsylvania, and continues s. to Carbondale, Scranton, and Wilkesbarre.

5. THE DELAWARE, LACKAWANNA & WESTERN R.R.

This is, like the Delaware & Hudson, one of the great coal companies of the country, and enters the State from its mines in Pennsyl-

vania by way of the Susquehanna, which it follows to Binghamton (1). See page 96. From here it sends out branches to Utica, Oswego, and

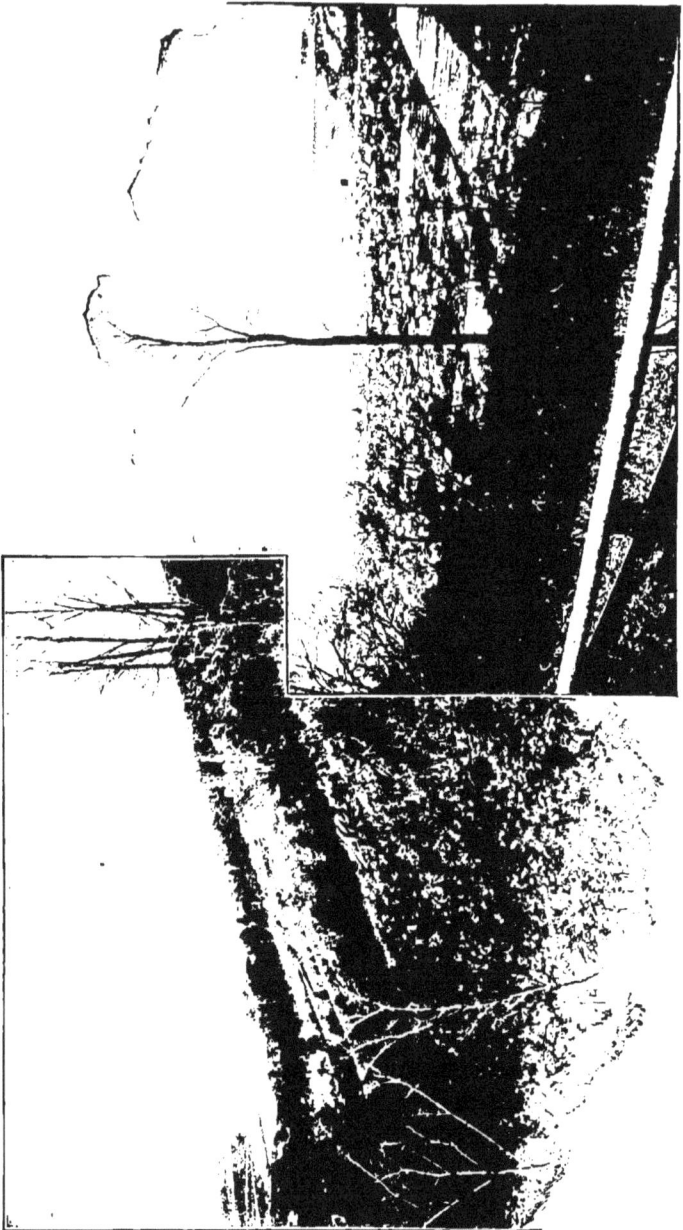

Buffalo, thus reaching by its own trains the central and western part of the State.

The Utica division follows up the Chenango River by Chenango Forks (2) and Greene, through the picturesquely situated village of Oxford (3), and through Norwich (4), a prosperous distributing-point, with iron and other manufactures; through Earlville (5) and on until just before reaching Waterville (6), the headquarters of hop-production, it passes over the watershed into the St. Lawrence system, and ends at UTICA (8). See page 83.

At Richfield Junction (7) a branch line runs through Bridgewater and West Winfield to Richfield Springs (25), for which see pages 57-59.

The Syracuse and Oswego division follow up the Tioughnioga from Chenango Forks (2), through Whitney's Point (9), and Marathon (10) to Tully (12), where Green Lake flows from the s. through the Tioughnioga into Chesapeake Bay, and from the N. through Onondaga Creek into the Gulf of St. Lawrence. See page 42.

Cortland (11) is at the junction of the two branches of the Tioughnioga, and at the confluence of 7 distinct valleys, separated by ranges of hills from 200 to 400 feet high, and radiating in different directions. This makes it the natural distributing-point for this entire region. It has also built up large manufactures, especially of carriages. A State Normal School is located here.

Two miles N. on the D. L. & W., and connected with Cortland by electric railway, is Homer, long noted for its excellent academy, and recently developing considerable manufactures.

The railway still rises, however, till it reaches a station called Summit, when it passes into the St. Lawrence system and descends rapidly to SYRACUSE (13). See page 81.

It follows down the s. side of Onondaga Lake, through the salt-covers, and crosses the Seneca River at Baldwinsville (14), a prosperous village with large flouring mills. It goes on down the Oswego River by Oswego Falls (15) and Fulton (see page 25), and ends at Oswego (16). See page 98.

The Buffalo division runs parallel with the Erie through Owego, Waverly, Elmira, Corning, and Bath to Atlanta (18). For this route see pages 96, 97.

From Owego (17), a branch road runs N. through Candor (25) and Caroline (26) to ITHACA (27), getting down the hill into the city by a series of criss-crosses quite puzzling to the inexperienced traveller. This city has already been spoken of as the seat of Cornell University (see page 35) and the centre of picturesque waterfalls (see page 48). It has also large manufactures, and besides its numerous railroads has a line of steamers down Cayuga Lake.

From Atlanta (18) the road bears off to the w., crosses the watershed, and enters the Genesee valley near Dansville (19). Two views of the valley from this place are given on the opposite page.

From here the railway strikes northwest to Mount Morris (20), crosses the Genesee, passes through Greigsville, where salt is taken out from mines 1200 feet deep at the rate of 800 tons a day, and curving around through Pavilion (21), at Alexander (22) comes near the Erie again and runs parallel with it into Buffalo (23).

6. THE LEHIGH VALLEY R.R.

A third great coal line also runs its lines into this State, and we may return by it from Buffalo (1). We observe that its route is by the central lakes, skirting Seneca and Owasco on one side, and Cayuga on both.

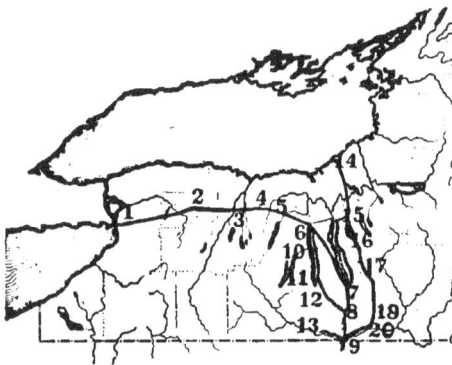

Starting from Buffalo (1), the road runs parallel with the New York Central to Batavia (2) (see page 78), and continues almost due E. to Rochester Junction (3), whence a branch runs N. to Rochester. It crosses the Auburn branch of the Central at Fisherville (4) and at Shortsville (5), and runs nearly parallel with it to Geneva (6). See page 81.

Here the main line crosses Seneca County, passing through Trumansburgh and Taughannock Falls to Ithaca (7). It then bears s. through Van Ettenville (8), passes out of the State at Waverly, and goes on to New York through Towanda, Mauch Chunk, and Allentown, Pa.

The western branch from Geneva (6) follows down the eastern shore of Seneca Lake, having connection with the main line from Willard Asylum (10) (see page 76). Ovid is on this connecting line, in the centre of the county. It goes on through Burdett (11) and Odessa (12), breaking off to the southeast to meet the main line at Van Ettenville (8). There is also a branch line from Waverly (9) to Elmira (13).

The Auburn division starts from Fair Haven (14), crosses the Central s. of the Seneca River, and from Auburn (15) follows up the outlet by Owasco Lake through Moravia (16), Groton (17), and Dryden, and curves around through Newark Valley (19) to Owego (20), whence it follows the Susquehanna to Waverly (9).

The Cayuga division crosses from Auburn (15) to Cayuga, and follows down the eastern shore of the lake through Union Springs and Aurora to Ithaca (7), where it connects with the main line.

At Aurora, one of the most beautiful villages in the State, is situated Wells College, a school of high rank for young ladies.

7. The Western New York & Pennsylvania R.R.

This is another of the roads connecting our New York cities with Pennsylvania. Its Pittsburgh division runs parallel with the Lake Shore tracks (see page 117) from Buffalo (1) through Angola (2) and Dunkirk (3) to Brocton (4), where it make a little circuit to the E. and strikes down to Mayville (5), at the head of Chautauqua Lake, and strikes s. through Sherman (6) to Corry, Pa., and thence on through Titusville to Oil City.

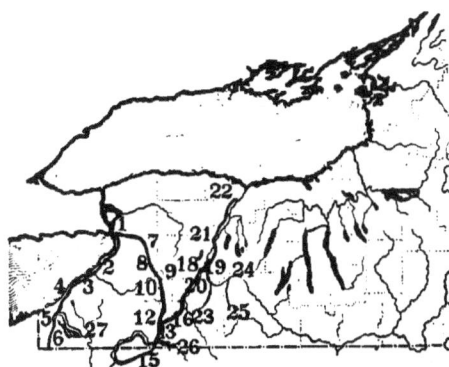

From Mayville a railway runs down the N. shore of Chautauqua to Jamestown.

The Buffalo division bears off to the s. of E. from Buffalo (1), turns to the s., passing through East Aurora (7) and Holland (8), cuts across a little corner of Wyoming County at Arcade (9), crosses the Buffalo, Rochester & Pittsburgh at Machias (10), follows the Ischua Creek down through Franklinville (11) to Hinsdale (12), and thence runs parallel with the Erie to Olean (13), and so on through Portville (14) to Emporium, with connections for Harrisburg, Philadelphia and Washington.

From Olean a narrow-gauge branch runs to Bradford, Pa. (15); another branch follows the s. branch of the Alleghany and circles back to Bradford.

The Rochester division runs from Olean (13) through Hinsdale (12) and Cuba (16) to Belfast (17), where it strikes the Genesee River, which it follows to Portage (18). Here it curves off to the E., connecting at Nunda (19) for Swain (20) at the junction of the Erie and the Central New York & Western. Near Mount Morris (21) it crosses the Genesee, and follows its western bank to Rochester (22). It is built upon the tow-path of the abandoned Genesee Valley Canal.

The Central New York and Western R.R. runs from Swain (20) s. to Angelica (23), and also E. to Wayland (24) and to Hornellsville (25).

Still another division runs from Olean through Portville to Bolivar (26), whence an extension not now operated connects with the other divisions at Angelica, and strikes w. to connect with the W. N. Y. & P. at Belfast.

8. THE NEW YORK ONTARIO & WESTERN R.R.

When this railway, then called the New York & Oswego Midland, was first projected, great things were expected of it. "See how it cuts

across the State," its advocates cried; "it is the hypothenuse of the triangle the New York Central takes two sides of." People forgot that it is no farther around a hill than over it, and invested in this line that went over the hills. So they lost their money, and the fast trains still go by the old routes. But to one who has leisure and enjoys picturesque scenery this line affords a delightful journey.

When Nicholas I. looked at the plans for the proposed railway from St. Petersburg to Moscow, he grew angry. "Why does it bend off here to the west?" he asked. "To pass through the city of Novgorod, your majesty." "And why these curves?" "To follow the Volga river, your majesty."— "And this twist?" "To avoid those mountains, your majesty."—"Get me a ruler!" The czar took it, put one end on St. Petersburg and the other on Moscow, and drew his pencil down the edge. "There is your railway from St. Petersburg to Moscow," he said. And almost in a straight line the railway runs for 400 miles.

But only czars make railways that way. The cost was enormous, and the road passed through only one large town. It was many years before a branch road was built to Novgorod.

It should be remembered in choosing a route that railway distances are measured not by miles but by hours. The West Shore has fewer miles between Buffalo and New York than the Central, but its quickest trains are some hours longer on the way. The experienced traveller learns to cling to the trunk routes, and to choose his trains not by maps but by time tables.

On the morning of Dec. 8, 1887, the author of this volume got up early enough to take at five o'clock the latest train from Barcelona in Spain by which he could catch his steamer home. At Gerona he got off for a cup of coffee. When he came back the train had started, and by a Spanish law seldom enforced he was seized by the two soldiers on guard and prevented from entering it. The station authorities had no French time tables and could tell him nothing as to trains beyond the frontier. He took the next train, a very slow one, and reached the frontier after dark. His ticket called for a change of cars, and a route nearly straight N. to Paris. But the train he was on went through to Marseilles, and on general principles he staid on it, riding all night, and being the next morning nearly as far from Paris as when he started. But he had reached the trunk line and the fast trains, he caught a special express that ran three times a week, and he got his steamer.

Starting from OSWEGO (1) and following the river to Fulton (2), the road bears off to the E. through Central Square (3), and follows the contour of Oneida Lake, passing through Cleveland (4) with its glass-works, and Fish Creek (5), a summer resort, and connecting with the New York Central and West Shore at Oneida (6) and Oneida Castle. It continues s. to Randallsville (7), where it connects for Rome (24) and Utica (25); and to Earlville (8) where it connects, by a road operated by the West Shore, for Syracuse (1). It runs nearly parallel with the D. L. & W. to Norwich (9), but crosses the Chenango and mounts the hill above Oxford (10), affording a delightful view.

At Clinton the Rome (24) branch connects with the branch from Utica (25). This beautiful village is the seat of Hamilton College and of Houghton Seminary.

Just before reaching Randallsville (7) the road passes through Hamilton, the seat of Colgate University.

At New Berlin Junction (11) it connects with its branch running up the Unadilla to New Berlin, and branching off northeast to Edmeston.

At Sidney (12) it crosses the D. & H., and curves around to Walton (13), on the West Branch of the Delaware, 1220 feet above tide.

The railway here mounts the hills of the divide between the Delaware and the Susquehanna system, which is 1800 feet at the highest point, beyond Franklin. This station is four miles from the village, which is delightfully situated in the Ouleout Valley, with water from artesian wells 365 feet deep. The Delaware Literary Institute is here.

From Walton (13) a branch runs up the Branch to Delhi (28), 1458 feet above tide, which is becoming a noted summer resort. By a stage ride of 8 miles up the river to Bloomville, one may make connection with the Ulster & Delaware R.R. See page 115.

It now curves to the southwest around the hills, nearly reaching the Delaware River at Hancock, and then turns at right angles, and runs nearly E. to the Sullivan county line. Through this county it bears southeast, passing through Liberty (18), a favorite health resort, especially for consumptives; and at Summitville (19) connecting for Ellenville (29), a charming village in the heart of the Shawangunk region on the D. & H. Canal. From this point on, see map on page 88.

From Hancock Junction the Scranton Division runs s. s. w. to Scranton, Pa.

Before reaching the Sullivan county line, the railway reaches Beaver Kil, a noted trout stream, and ascends it, following the bank closely, beyond Parksville, 1582 feet above tide. It then crosses the watershed into the Mongaup valley, and crosses the Neversink beyond Fallsburgh, and the D. & H. Canal just before reaching Summitville. Between Mountain Dale and Summitville the road descends 420 feet in 8 miles, from 962 to 542 feet above tide.

The railway at Wurtsboro (compare map on page 92), passes out of the Mamakating Valley, pierces the Shawangunk mountains by a tunnel 3800 feet long, and reaches Bloomingburgh, celebrated by Washington Irving in his "Hans Schwartz". In the colonial period this was a frontier town, and suffered much from Indian raids. It is 757 feet above the sea.

From MIDDLETOWN (20) it runs nearly due E. across the county through Campbell Hall (21) to Cornwall (22), whence it turns s. and at Weehawken (23) connects with the ferry for New York.

9. HARLEM DIVISION *of the N. Y. C. & H. R. R.R.*

This road runs through the eastern valley of the watershed of which the Hudson river is the western valley, a region in many respects more like New England than like the rest of New York. See map on page 88.

Starting from the Grand Central Depot in New York it runs past Bedford Park, with beautiful Bronx Park opposite; on through Mount Vernon and past the marble quarries of Tuckahoe to White Plains, where the battle of Oct. 28, 1776 was fought. It goes on through Kensico, Chappaqua, Mount Kisco, Bedford, and Katonah ; has a branch circuit from Golden's Bridge to Brewsters, famed for its iron mines, by Lake Mahopac and through Carmel ; passes through Patterson and Pawlings in a delightful valley especially charming at Amenia ; reaches the junction of three States at Boston Corners, curves to the w. at Hillsdale, and to the N. before reaching Philmont ; and ends at Chatham.

Here its connections are by the Boston & Albany to Hudson, and to Albany on the w.; and on the E. through Pittsfield, Mass., to Springfield, Worcester and Boston ; and by the Lebanon Springs R.R. to Lebanon Springs, and, crossing the Fitchburg at Petersburg Junction, to Bennington, Vt.

From Niverville a road runs to Hudson, passing through the most beautiful part of the county, especially near Stuyvesant Falls

The New York & Northern division of the Central runs between the Harlem and the Central, starting at 155th street, New York, and running through to Brewsters. It is not shown on the map.

The three great trunk lines E. are I. the Fitchburg, connecting with the West Shore at Rotterdam Junction, and with the Central at Troy, and passing through Mechanicsville, Eagle Bridge, and the great Hoosac Tunnel, 4⅓ miles long and costing 20 millions, to Fitchburg and Boston ; II. the Boston & Albany, just spoken of; and III. the New York & New Haven, starting from New York and following along the shore through New Rochelle and Port Chester.

10. THE ULSTER & DELAWARE R.R.

This picturesque line starts from Kingston, strikes the Beaver Kil at West Hurley, follows it down nearly to its junction with Esopus Creek, and then follows up the Creek through Phœnicia, Shandaken and Big Indian, to its source near the boundary of the county, crosses the watershed at Grand Hotel on the county line, and descends into the Delaware system, reaching at Arkville the lowest point on the railroad in the county, 1344 feet above tide. The village of Margaretville is 1½ miles from here, and Andes 12 miles. See map on page 88.

The road now ascends the East Branch of the Delaware to the N., passing through Roxbury. It crosses into the Hudson system again as it curves, but regains the Delaware at Stamford, the prettiest village in the Catskills, and follows it through Hobart to Bloomville. A stage-ride of 8 miles down the river to Delhi connects this road with the N. Y. O. & W. (see page 113).

From Phœnicia there is a branch line to Hunter, and to the Catskill Mountain House, making this a delightful route by which to visit the Catskills. Slide Mountain, shown on page 17 is reached by a stage-ride of 11 miles from Big Indian. This view of Delaware County is taken from Grand Hotel, 1886 feet above tide water.

Stamford is almost at the junction of three of the great river systems. It is on a branch of the Delaware, the streams a little way w. begin to flow into the Susquehanna, and Bear Creek, one mile E. empties into the Schoharie.

The following elevations in this county are given in French's Gazetteer: Delaware River, at E. border 830 ft.; junction of two branches 922;

Hancock 943; Hale's Eddy 950; Deposit 1004; Sidney 1010; Franklin 1240; Arkville 1345; Stamford 1765; Elk Creek Summit 1859; Davenport Centre 1898; Mt. Pisgah, near Andes 3400.

11. WALLKILL VALLEY R.R.

This starts from Campbell Hall, shown in the map on page 88, and follows the Wallkill branch of Rondout Creek. It curves to the northeast at Montgomery; passes through Walden, where there is manufacture of English cutlery; Wallkill, where 30,000 quarts of milk a day are used in summer by the New York Condensed Milk Co.; and New Paltz, the site of a State Normal School, and the station for Lake Mohonk (see page 41) and Lake Minnewaska; soon crosses the Wallkill and then bears straight N., crossing the Rondout on an iron bridge 150 feet high and 960 feet long at Rosendale, noted for its cement; and then turning off to the northeast to Kingston. See map on page 88.

12. THE ELMIRA, CORTLAND AND NORTHERN R.R.

Starting from Camden (1), on the R. W. & O. (see page 99) this road strikes S. from McConnellsville (2), nearing the E. shore of Oneida Lake, to Canastota (3), on the New York Central; passes through Cazenovia (4) and DeRuyter (5); and crosses the D. L. & W. at Cortland (6), for which see page 109. Thence it bears southwest to Ithaca (7), for which see page 109; curves around to the southeast through Caroline (8), and Candor (9); turns W., passing through Spencer and Van Ettenville (10), and at Horseheads (11) turns S. again to Elmira (12).

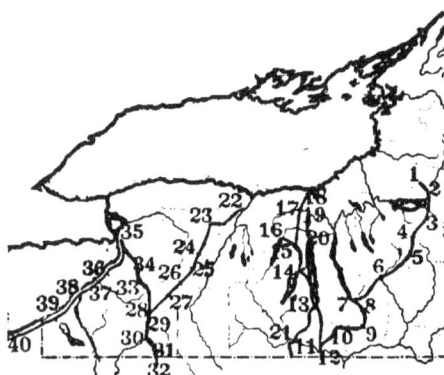

13. THE PENNSYLVANIA R.R.

This great corporation controls a single line across the State, still usually referred to as the Northern Central. Striking N. from the Susquehanna at Williamsport, Pa., it runs from Elmira (12) through Horseheads (11) and so on through Havana (now Montour Falls) to Watkins (13), for which see pages 35, 45. Following up Seneca Lake for a few miles, it bears off northwest to Keuka Lake at Penn Yan (14), and thence circles around by Stanley (15) to Canandaigua (16), where it connects by the New York Central for Rochester.

From Stanley (15), a branch runs N. through Newark (17), on the Central and the West Shore, to Sodus Point (18), thus giving the Pennsylvania road a harbor on Lake Ontario.

14. THE FALL BROOK RAILWAY

This road was built to give the Fall Brook coal mines an outlet in

New York. It connects with the New York Central at Lyons (19), and runs s. through Geneva (20), by the w. shore of Seneca Lake, to Watkins (13), crossing the Pennsylvania at Himrods Junction and running w. of it. It then bears off southwest to Corning (21), and runs s. to its mines at Blossburg. Pa.

A branch line runs across from Dresden to Penn Yan.

15. THE BUFFALO, ROCHESTER & PITTSBURGH R.R.

This line starts from Rochester (22), curves to the southeast to LeRoy (23), and then strikes nearly s. through Warsaw (24) to Silver Lake junction (25), when it turns off to the southwest again, through Bliss (26) and Machias Junction (27) to Ashford (28), whence it goes s. through Ellicottville (29), to Salamanca (30) and Limestone (31) to Bradford.

From Ashford (28) the Buffalo division runs northwest through Springville (33) and Colden (34) to Buffalo (35).

16. THE LAKE SHORE & MICHIGAN SOUTHERN R.R.

This finely equipped western route follows the shore of Lake Erie from Buffalo (35) through Angola (36), Silver Creek (37), Dunkirk (38), and Westfield (39), through Erie, Pa., (40) and so on to Chicago through Cleveland and Toledo.

17. THE NEW YORK, CHICAGO & ST. LOUIS (NICKEL PLATE) R.R.

This road runs parallel with the Lake Shore through New York, with a connection at Westfield (39) for Mayfield and Chautauqua Lake.

18. THE DUNKIRK, ALLEGHENY VALLEY & PITTSBURGH R.R.

This road, leased by the New York Central, starts s. from Dunkirk (38), passes through Fredonia (see page 98), and Lily Dale, by the beautiful Cassadaga Lake (41), and through Sinclairville (42), crosses the Erie at Falconer (43), and after passing through Frewsburgh crosses the State line beyond Fentonville, and terminates at Titusville. Pa.

19. THE LONG ISLAND R.R.

This road now controls all the railways on the island, and is sufficiently shown in the map on the following page. The distance from New York to Greenport is 94 miles : to Sag Harbor 100 miles.

For what is said of the towns on Long Island see pages 59, 60. For the new bridge that will connect the Long Island railway with New York see pages 51, 62. The summer traffic of some of these lines nearest New York is enormous, as the southern coast of the island gives the inhabitants of New York and its adjoining cities delightful sea air and bathing within a few minutes' ride.

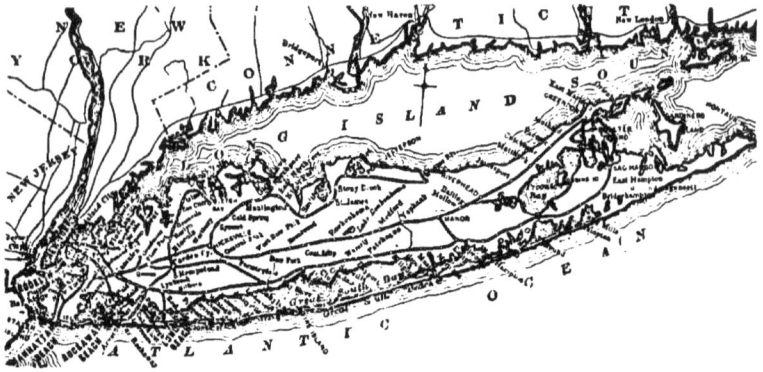

INDEX

INDEX

www.ingramcontent.com/pod-product-compliance
Lightning Source LLC
Chambersburg PA
CBHW030614270326
41927CB00007B/1179